MALLARME

Paul Fearne

chipmunkapublishing
the mental health publisher

All rights reserved, no part of this publication may be reproduced by any means, electronic, mechanical photocopying, documentary, film or in any other format without prior written permission of the publisher.

>Published by
>Chipmunkapublishing
>United Kingdom

http://www.chipmunkapublishing.com

Copyright © 2020 Paul Fearne

ISBN   978-1-78382-569-1

MALLARME

This book is a work of prose poetry. It is addressed to the 19th century French poet Stephane Mallarme.

And in addition;

Each paragraph of this book is a self-contained fragment of a larger poetic whole.

Paul Fearne

MALLARME

Mallarme, there was once a time, in the middle of this, that had fire and laughter, but now only has tears. But do not be afraid. There are more things here than we had dreamed. Do not be alarmed, there is much to do.

And then, in solemn night, there comes a blessing. It is not what the sands of hope had relinquished, nor what the borrowed time had come to. It is more than all of this, all of this put together.

Mallarme, do we see our strides as being of levity, or of silk? I have no sense of the day, so I cannot tell. There are new things to take in here. There are old things to be sure of. We must not walk here – we will run.

In the middle of a great sentence, we let go of our departure, and know the floor to be a thing cherished. Maybe there will be something more as a result of all this. Maybe, in time, something will come to be cherished here.

Mallarme, are you the one to tell teachers, yes, they can achieve greatness? Are you the one to shine the light? Guide the way, and have your say. There is nothing more in this, so let us depart with a wink. It can be done.

There is a noise here. It comes from some other place. It does not come from us, but from the great beyond. What have we found in the timing of things, is not of the earth, but of the solstice, and all she wants.

There is pleasure here, my Mallarme, but I just can't get to it. In the spring, yes I know, it is lovely isn't it. But when we swing from branch to branch, there is a harmony that is hardly there.

Moisture in the wind. Sand on the grain. We have fibres in the swim of it. Do not be the one to shirk, Mallarme. Only be the one to catch the swimming school, and there will be much frivolity.

A throw of the dice, indeed Mallarme. Yours is the sunlight, as ours in the vanquishing of night. Be a troubadour in an all that you do. And here, where the sunlight does not fold – again.

Light and sparkles – we see no difference. But there is some subtle differences in the weave and fibre of these things. Light and sparkles. They have inside them both, what must not be touched.

And now, in the silence, Mallarme, you work, and know how to be host of so much. Your Tuesday Gatherings, your Mardis, were a light and a beacon. There is more to say here, and we will say it.

The distance between this hat and the next, is like a fawning and a nerve. You had the nerve, alright, and sometimes it became a nervous complaint, that at one stage got you a year of your teaching duties, Mallarme.

There is something that does not act as the forlorn, nor as the rose thorn in the night. Be a true longing to the song of the twilight, and yours will be the out shining of light from deep within.

The whisper of things is not what we should expect from something so enamoured with its own breath. Things are not envisaged in this way, and so they should be told where to sit, and nothing else.

MALLARME

Mallarme, a feeling I once had, that the tempest was here for us to see it through. Do you understand me, my sweet Mallarme? Do you see into those crevices that do not let in the time, let alone the day?

I will put here, Mallarme, anything you want from me. I will put my name in fire, and loosely dredged fibres. There is more than can be said of us, I believe, my dear man, so sit here, and loosen things with salt, and speak of a time for ours, yes.

The time it takes to meander through the woods, is not our time, Mallarme. The breathing heart, and the sign of ages, have gathered for a rendition of the template as it falls in a sense to us all.

You are not asking enough, Mallarme. You have more to ask, so ask it. There is more to be done, and some to be left undone. Be sure in yourself Mallarme, be sure, and then continue.

All the more reason to keep going. We have no reasons, no reasons but the blind compulsion that follows each of us to the grave. This is my journey, one that I cannot even take pleasure in.

One two three, upwards, and through. Mallarme do you succumb to this plight of ours? Do you see the night for what it is? There is something more here, something we can play with, and be taught by.

There is something here, that none of us comprehend. Something that the wind sees, and the sparrow knows, but that is all. There can only be this, and this alone. So come for it, and be glad.

Mallarme, what have you? What has the night? What has the day? What have you and me, as we come once again for the distilling of dreams through blackest depths. What have we!

A thousand encounters, with this, that and the other. A thousand turns, a thousands ways to be. A thousand remonstrations at the unfairness of it all. And then, simple a thousand aptitudes, and let it be.

Mallarme does the sky turn for you? Do things move in your direction? Do you send for fire, and get back rocks? Is this where our torments cease? Do we know what time it will be tomorrow?

Watching things as they spread. Watching things, as a new flock wheel and dive. Believing that the moisture of the stars is ours. Feeling like things will right themselves.

Eventually, if the night is right, and the feeling of camaraderie strong enough, there comes an action to pull the beats of life, out of their very core. Mallarme, do you see again? Are you the one to see?

Eventually, there comes a corner stone to life. Eventually, there is more than enough to signal the day. Eventually, there comes a common place acceptance of things. In the sense we have between this and that – that.

Mallarme, have we come to that concluding bark – that strip of willow that has only the feelings and pulses of generality. When we look – there it is found. When we look – there it is found.

MALLARME

Considering that we have never been in this situation, it is working out like an indelible sheet on beds of grey. There can only be one thing we must do – and that is come up for air, one more time, and breathe that deeper breath.

Hark back to the time we had. Wasn't it just like the feelings of strangers? Mallarme, have you felt this? Have you felt like a stranger in a strange land? Let us look that one last time.

Like the new, that we once knew, that was in lieu, counter-wise. See these things, as a draw string, that only comes back once. There is time to settle old scores, and be with something we truly treasure.

Look for something greater. Mallarme, do you hear me? Look for something in the now – I tell you old friend. But do not do away with things, not yet, at least. Watch for the feast, and let it come.

Fortitude, there is no favour. Fortresses are built on less. Do us the favour of your existence. There has never been a time like this. We come to do good, and here we stand.

Mallarme, my old friend. Do justice to our visage. Do justice to the sound of our motion. You are one to be prone to things. Prone to be feathers in autumn light. There is nothing else.

Cajoling the sun to rise – that is a rite – a rite of spring. Never before have so many souls been so in harmony with what is not. Do not bother us, sweet brother, there will be time enough.

Let us be, to waste to the bottom, and then up again, and fighting fit, and through and up and away. Mallarme, this much is told – we will make it to the end, where all things are possible.

What is it that we want? What is that you want, my friend? What is the way of it – so we can remember, and tell our children, and they may have a memory of it. So up we come, in sweet delight, and then down, to the ground, and through.

Mallarme, do not believe in the sand – it is not for us. Believe in something with a more sturdy vantage, like the moon, or the stars. Be the person to trade in windows for frost. And then we will know.

The things that do not die. Be like the wind, it does not die. Be like the shards of glass that do not litter. Be like the sun, its motion is assured. Be like the clouds who dance around the sky.

And then, without care, or rhyme nor reason, Mallarme comes, and treats each person he meets to a poem, of vast obscurity or vast innovation. Each of us, come, and be sure of ourselves.

What have we now, but the little things. What have we now, but the things that charge ahead. What have we now, but the vanquishing of tears on snow. We will survive to see another dawn.

Mallarme, what is next? Do you see your bottles of life stacked up against the wall, always coming down? There is never anything to chase here. There is never the creed to lay on the ground.

MALLARME

Feeling like it is past the time of calculations. A feeling like no other. A feeling like we are on our way, and the first gates have been passed. Like we said, a feeling like no other.

All that is put to rest. All that we see, but don't feel. All that, you, Mallarme, are left to deal with. You got married in England, but then had to ratify your marriage in France so that you daughter would not be considered illegitimate.

Forging ahead – there is no time, there is no place. What we thought was the end, is only the beginning. What we thought was its difficulty, is only what lets it stir. Be the mane, it will suit you.

Overhead, underfoot. There is no way forward. Underfoot, overhead. We can go forward if we think in checks. Overhead, and underfoot. Mallarme, do you dream. Are you dreaming now?

There is a place, like no other – there is a place that does not turn an inch. Is it for us to decide where to go next? Is it a calling to the wind that harrows the way? Can we really believe it?

Raging through the whispers, there is a neverness here that does not flinch. Not a single backward step. Mallarme, have you seen your life to date? Have you witnessed its dis-ease? You have won Mallarme.

Holding on, there is nothing left. Holding on, there is one small piece of it that has fallen. There is a time here like no other. A chance to breathe again the breath of a thousand nights labour.

Looking backwards, we cannot see. Looking forwards, we cannot see. Looking to the left, the right. All we see is mist. But Mallarme – can you see, from your vantage, all that comes to pass?

Gaining in depth, there is a way forward. It sings no easy way. It barks, and bleats like the start of another sound. There is nothing ordinary about this sound, and in it there is fate.

Mallarme, is this the way, the way to your heart? Do you come to us when we are ready, and willing, to be your apprentice? Do things come smoothly to you, even when times are hard?

What is not at issue, are the things which poured from your pen. They are sublime. What is not at issue, is your life as you led it (on the whole). These things do not concern us.

Have no more to say, Mallarme. Have the wind at your back. Have the steel on your shoulder, have all things that do not go. Have what is most at stake, and that is life. Indeed, have it all, yes.

Look at that. There is a prize here for the first person to be prepared to spell their name in gold leaf, in half the time it has taken me to write these words. How long is that? We do not know.

There is in this wind, a sort of calm, wouldn't you agree, Mallarme? There is in this sky, a sort of delight. There is now, in every cloud that cuts its way, a new found belief.

What is in the moon, is not for us. What we savour in the longing for things, is not our longing. There dreams in every one of us a sort of new found departure. Newly found, and newly won.

Catching on fire. This levity is the shower's as a late storm comes in to render the flames into sodden dust. And here, we sing that one more time, and know our time to be a worthy one.

In the middle of the trumpet call there exists a light that has no features. There exists in this call nothing to let us be by. And when we see ourselves under the light of a moonlit sky, Mallarme, nothing.

Mallarme, do you see the fortress for what it is? Do you see the way from here? I have to say you do, given what I know of you. There are trees waiting to see your journey again.

What is in the tempest is not what we expected. What we expected was something of the arcane, but its centre is full rich with silent edges. We can search for this treasure in no other place.

Come forth, Mallarme, you are wanted in all quadrants. Is this your style? Is this what we thought it would be? The times are here for the leaving still, and that is time enough.

When we fought for our lives, we really fought. When we sang in guarded breath, we really sang. There is not often a way through these things, but we have found a way. This much is sure.

There are ways to be, and ways not to be. In this life, we chose our way, and are thus chosen for the victory that is in us all. There can be no other way. As always, up and around.

There are things, Mallarme, that do not disguise. There are lights that hold onto the night. And in this, we weep a tear, and have at our disposal more than the flying of fireflies in summer's dream.

The luckiest, are the few. These few harness what the world would rather not be, and then, with encasement in hand, tell of a dream that is for the ages. Let it go, I hear you say.

Mallarme, do not talk here. To talk here is to break the covenant of the senses. That is okay though, because in the mist, where the sands do not go, there is easily enough to be met.

What is here, oh one? Mallarme, is this you? Is this you unto plains of golden silk? I should hope so, I have waited for you in times of treasured seek. Be nice, it will suit you.

What is this furthest thing? What is the time it takes to a feather in the night? I have no more questions – no this is not true. I have many more questions, and I will ask them.

Mallarme, do you find yourself in tiers of gold? Do you find yourself incumbent by the meadow? There will be no time to seek, as we have been doing. Only time to silence the night, and all she has.

The thought of it, shoots spires of reluctance into everything we do. But that is okay, we need not speak of our adventures, only touch their souls from time to time. Yes, this is it.

MALLARME

The long haul, and the dreams of borrowed men. What is it that we seek? What is it that we have never known, and have now caught a glimpse of? There is nothing left, my dear one.

Mallarme – you were working in your school, and you had some poems published in a certain collection, and so enraged some of the parents, you had to move schools! It was a collection of the Parnassians.

When the sails tread the shore, there is nothing left for us to do. When we have seen the last of it, the night-time avenges our sight, and we come again for the fight. Do not deceive us, we are free.

And now, my dear Mallarme, we see what we want to see, and know what we want to know. And then, like a flash of light, there comes an insight, into those things that have no soul, or will to fight.

The chances we take with our lives are enough to sullen the curtain on any play we come to mention. And here, what is left, is nothing other than all. We will not take more, there is no choice.

The sky – the vast sky, Mallarme. What have we thought but all, what have we found but the sense of things. There is a troupe that is not worth their name on the bill. But they come, and we watch.

The daylight is not one to spark a fire. But what we see when we come out in the day, is not what we would have expected. What we see is more than enough. More than enough to be.

Ransoming the tethers of forgetfulness. We lie in wait for all that is, and then when we are hurried from this place to the next, a new beginning, in this or that adventure. Mallarme, are you tired of it?

What a waste is the night. What a piece of wanton mist. There is no deeper moat. No feeling more alive than what is happening now. Mallarme, do you feel yourself slipping into the daylight?

There are times that cannot be shown. There are ways that have as their assistance the mighty bells of consistency. Be one with your desire – but let it fall. And here, do not subside.

The wrong way is up. The wrong way is down. The only way is through. And that leaves a scar the size of a leopard. So let us be besieged, and come down of our vantage to see the contest.

All the more reason to come forth. There is a load of simplicity here – we must not lean. Mallarme, do you hike? Do you swim the Hellespont? There is no more than this.

What is this life? – how does it work? What are its attributes? There is no more time to see into things. We are welling up with moisture – we must not care. We must only care. That is what we must do.

Here, in the ocean, as far as the tide will take us, there is a place my dear Mallarme. We find it, and never let go of it. Even the tide cannot bring another. Be at bliss, we know what to do.

MALLARME

Lying straight. Supine. Always believing in things. Never throwing a stone in anger. Never being that one to shirk. The in-between of things cannot stop us. We will go to the edge, just to see.

All the more willing. There are difficulties that charge their glasses. All this is fun, but what of the reality. It comes in gushing force – as you do Mallarme. Just sit with it – it will be gone.

Seeing the evolution of things – of this to that. There can never be more of satisfying lull. And when it comes, all things are well, for that one moment, and then on again, into life.

Mallarme, what is this for? What is this journey for? Who forsakes who? Is there a meaning in this rhyme? So come now, do not be the one to tether up the keepsake. It will not be pleased.

Glad to be ensconced in it. Its yearning is a thing not hinted at in books of ancient memory. And when we lift our head, we know something new, and something old, and something in-between.

Mallarme, do you see the stars? They are the ones we have been looking for all these years. And now we see more than we ever have. What is this – do we feel it? Yes we do.

Yes, and in the way of things. There is now, something very close. There is now something closer than before. We will wait, and then see what we will see. Yes, again.

The time we spend working in this or that way, is not what we had expected. There are times to send, and times to be sent. There was never once a thing, my dear Mallarme, that was taken as ballast. Yes.

And here, where we are left to linger, more timely adhesions from the mist – we must do all we can to forget. But we must remember! This is true in all the ways of being in tune. Yes.

The vibrancy of colour here. The colours do not meld into one, Mallarme, they are sharp and still sharp. What is it that we thought we would say here? Up, and across. Up and across.

A nestled speed comes from the rung. And then, without care, nor reason, there exists a plight of all people's lingering like a desolate farmland, on arches of parchment. We must away.

Mallarme, can we ever get out of the way of things? Can we ever still ourselves to the core, and abound in nature's victory over time? There are things to see here, and then some.

The running into things. We talk here, and have our say. But what of the night – she is angry. Angry at the way things are handled. But we must not run, we must only say our way, and be the one who laughs, but a little.

There are cautions to the unwary here. Cautions to be headed in darkened places. Cautions to offered by the sea, the sea, who has seen so much. Mallarme, will you see with us?

The task at hand, is not a simple one. We have the gradient of sand to keep us company. We have the land itself, which will never yield. And we have the sky, oh mighty goddess.

MALLARME

The guiding buoy who does deliver. Delivers the map which we all need. Delivers the directions, and the song. Delivers what is required, and then Mallarme, something more besides.

There was never a mightier thing than this. This thing that has no wings, nor means of propulsion. It lingers in places of respite, to come at the speed between pinions. It is of this earth.

And your return to Paris, Mallarme, you became a socialite. Your Tuesday gatherings – aplomb. Your friendship with Manet, a godsend. And then the rest. A time for pleasure.

The wind is strong here. It barks no bite. But what of the signs of things? What of these things, in themselves? We march on roads of untroubled tread, and here gather ourselves for the after.

A fast moving horse, who carries the world. There is no one to see it, nor hear its mighty nay. Mallarme, do you follow, on crimson steeds, that know of no bounds, but the world's?

Catching the song of a bird who only knows one tune. It is the tune of everything, that ever was. How will we find it again? Only in the arbour of sweetness will we find it again.

Mallarme – do not be alarmed. There is nothing to be afraid of here. There is only the time we have, as it whittles away. There is only the noise we make to keep things at bay.

What is surer now than ever was, is that the time it takes to settle a night's wager, is no time at all. You see, 'A throw of the dice will never abolish chance'. This much we know, Mallarme.

The distance between this wing, and the next, is not enough to see us fly. For us to fly, we must right ourselves, and truly imagine what flying would be like. And then one, two, three, away.

There are times amongst it, times that have the suitability of timeless bastions. Mallarme, are you lost to us? Are you the one who does not renege? Listen closely, it is here.

Having more than what can be conceived. Having the dice, and throwing them. Having what is left in the sand. Being told to go, and going. In the interim, a force beyond our control.

Forests that staple shut. All the more reason. Going for a new signature, and having it rub. Mallarme, do you feel the pull of it? Do you feel how much of it is here? More than the temperature of gods.

There are things we must not see. There are things we must only see. And then, when we have seen, we run, and have our tales chased by what can never be thrown.

Mallarme, you are here for me. You are the one who scales on might and purpose. What can never remind us of, is all that can be, and all that will be. Much relinquishing comes.

Further than ever before. There are no words to describe this. No words to hunt down in distant silk, and worn down places. Come for the play, and stay for the day. Will you?

MALLARME

Mallarme, will you be the one who languishes on chosen ruins? Do you see yourself in plaintive song? What is there left, but the chosen smile of the west wind. Come to us, we will wait.

Having the time of it. Having what is left. Having the need we have, and letting it be conquered. Mallarme, do you hear nothing more than in what is travelling past? I should hope so.

What disperses with the wind. What is here, but never found. Coming closer, but then circling back. Being torn asunder, but somehow living to tell the tale. And when we need it most – life, and all that it brings.

Mallarme are you the one who sees the way? I should hope so, you are sitting in your chair here as if you know something. But should we come to you for wisdom, oh man of letters? We shall see.

A treasure we never thought of. A flight to realms majestical. Carry the furnace, you will not burn. Carry the furnace, and all things will be well. There is nothing left here, but simply to say – yes.

Mallarme, are your sounds the sounds of ages? Are you ready to move at any time? This much comes to us, and we seek further shores as a result. Be further in the sense of it, and you will see.

The timelessness of it all. We find ourselves anew, in each new footstep to the sublime. Mallarme, will you be with us as we walk to the palace. We will walk, and not run.

A closing in on things, things that have no speed. There are times that have no continuity, and times that do. What is not lost to us, is in the way we breathe each breath.

Mallarme, have you won, or have you lost? Your life does not tell the tale. But that is fine as we see ourselves again in timeless grandeur, and with our feet surely planted on the ground.

What more is there to know of you, my dear Mallarme. Your teaching suffered because of your literary undertakings, but what of your life? You muddled through, and tried not to be overwhelmed.

And then, and there, a new way to be. What has crossed us will no longer cross us. And here, where we are in the hands of something stronger, a new force will beckon. Yes.

And here, Mallarme, we have launched ourselves into the outer realms of thought and time and do not know which way to go. And here we will be the languished, to your side hope.

Never missing a beat. Always somewhere, never here. Aforementioned, but with a difference. We love to be that thing that barks your name. And then, refreshed, we come.

All we can say, is all we can be. All we are driven for, is all that we can say. And then, as the mound grows slowly bigger, there is a chance to gauge ourselves against the best.

Mallarme, do you have lessons in feeling, so that you may come to life, and know how to express yourself immediately. I hope so, because such is the demand, that there should be such things.

MALLARME

Wind, and rain. Strong wind, and strong rain. Sheets of rain, and bitter wind. These are but a few of the niceties we experience, and then, a lark. We have not the wind in us to believe such things.

Mallarme, come forth, do not hesitate, do not relinquish, do not fall on bygone times. We will see you anew, and know you to be a feather in a dark time. We turn to you now.

Whether or not you can be with us, we beg your acceptance. And here where we lie in earth uplifting, there will come a new sort of delay, that needs time as its essence, and foraging for its light.

Mallarme, are you here to bother, or are you here to swim? You are here for neither, and that much is okay. Will you prattle a little for us, to be who you want. Be cold, we will oblige.

The highest peak – there is no air to breathe, so we come down in raging torrents. We love the thing that does not want. And here where the sun does not shine, and the moon does not burn, a respite.

Coming back down to the distant shore. We are like a new family, all made of gold. Never before have we seen the running water move so rapidly. But that is okay, there is more than enough.

Loaded in, about face, a look of square. Do not be one to sit on the shards, they will only impress. Mallarme, can you run with us – can you stave off the past long enough for us to enter.

A fear I once had – that I would be alone, in times unending.
Well no more, we have not seen the times look so voracious,
that they eat sideways, and back, and through. Yes, and
then...

Mallarme, can you see the sense we have. The sense of a
thousand dreamless nights. There is here, something we
should only hint at, for dreams are precious, and should be
had every night.

The wasting of winter sand. There is no place like this, as we
quickly jump down wooded peaks. And then, like a wind that
knows no burden, true to sailing wind, there is hope.

Mallarme, do we have the heart, the heart to hold on? There
can only be one thing to remind us of the cold, and that is
the now as it envisages half-seen remnants of times past.

In the middle of things, there are chances to be alight to the
day. And then, when we fetch a pitcher of water to douse
what is left, there will come another beacon to remonstrate
by.

What can never be said in the seam of things. What can only
be said, has been said. And here, where we lounge once
again against a hollowing base, time, and a little respite.

Ranging through like a mass of iron. We see ourselves in
the mirror and know that time has passed. And then, when
we figure the result to the cause, we harbour no remorse.

All the more reason to settle the scores of a thousand hope
filled nights. We are the ones to land here. We are the ones

MALLARME

to be right in amongst it. And then, over, like a storm in summer.

Come for the playing, Mallarme, come for the mist as it disperses. There is never a rounding-out of the soul here. Never a living, breathing, festive cheer, that has as its wake the more anon.

Having a guess at all that is. It is a mighty holler, one that we never thought could happen by the light of the moon. There is now a new bow to string – will you help? I hope so.

Mallarme, the sea is rising, and it rises to take us with it. We will only go upon one condition – that the flow is fast, and without dominion. And here we are, through and roundabouts.

A considerable poesy greets our arrival. And here there comes a mighty sound. It is the sound of you and me as we stage once again for the lark and the peregrine. Do not be here, the mist will takes us.

The lavish wear of the moonlit dice. Mallarme, you translated Poe, just as Baudelaire did! You were an English teacher after all. You even gave a lecture tour in Brussel's! And to mixed reports!

The harvest that only sings. The newness of a fading flower. What we find when we raise our heads is not often what we find. Come for the garden. It beckons to you, as you will see.

Mallarme, do this one thing. Raise your hat above your head, and shake it back and forth. And you see, a new found longing greets us all. And then, when enough is enough – something more.

A fortunate landing on soft ground. There is never anything to saddle up against, except this. And what is this, but the limb of an ancient tree, that has known the years of a century.

Mallarme, do we sing again? De we have the method to right the ship? Is there enough of the perfunctory in our movements to let our minds run free? Mallarme, come.

Listening closely, we find ourselves rallied in silk. Do not be obliged here, I hear you say. All we must do is ask the question, and low, we are new. And low, we hear again.

The mighty and the plain. Feeling like tomorrow, Mallarme - feeling like we knew it would rain. Having the saddle without the horse. We will make it to our respective homes.

Forging ahead, without time for the newness of it all. We come in time for lunch, and eat our fill. And here, where the lot is of the bristle, we move in unison through the hills.

Overcoming again, we see our lives as vessels in the rain that has not stopped in one hundred years. Mallarme, as she comes in crimson silk, there can be no time to wander.

A new found wish that has nothing to give. And here, as in everywhere, a fight for the bravest to renew our hope in times of gold. There is never enough to linger, so on we move.

Coming in light and shade. There is a feeling we all once had, that the times are near the end, but up we come again, and despite our very selves, we move forward again, and again.

Mallarme, do you squander your combined yearning on things unreal. I have felt a newness that does not transpire, it only sits and weaves and languishes in the mean-time.

There was once a chance that had no steel. No favour to bestow, no predilection to devour. The sense we have to hurry on fate, and belittle what it is that holds us back. We will win.

Mallarme, have you seen the performance? – Do you know what we are all talking about? There is a sense in the longing, there is trust in the sea. There can never be anything more than this.

What have we fought for? What have the days been so inclined to say? When there was once the time left, we have the scurrying of fireflies in night. Be one with the sand dunes, it will help.

Mallarme, have you heard the rain as it patters on ancient rooves? There is never a side-glimpsed hope of it. And here, where we look again, new finds, and newer obstacles.

A wish that we all have, that the time it takes to make amends is not a distance made in hours or days, but in weeks. And then, when we are through with it, a sound, one that never leaves.

There can only be one outcome for all of this. And that is to sing the riotous blast evenly, with covers of never ending dew. The morning will then have us, Mallarme, yes.

Hoary, and without care. There is never a smoother ride that
this. And when we come for the rain, there is a portion that is
left behind. Do not worry, it will not last. We will be here.

Mallarme, do you see the light? Can you touch the burning?
Is there enough filament to fill the box? When we see in
times of duress, we see a larger picture, one that can never
be erased.

Watch for the forest, as we ride past. The sun gleams
through, and the morning mist has not yet departed.
Something strange is about to happen to us, but that is fine,
it will not hurt.

Mallarme, are you the one to see the columns of delight as
they sing the music of the spheres? We cannot sense
anything otherwise. And then, without care, a new glimpse of
what is said.

Gaining in momentum, there is a chance that sighs will dim,
and what has caused so much pain will come again to take
us there. But what have we thought but otherwise, yes.

Mallarme, are you stronger than this? Are you the rising of
solemn tides on back on respite? There can only be what is
next, and in that there will be wonder on the lips of the sea.

Calling from the wild, new daring, new shards to claw. There
is a mighty semblance that can only see in times of heart –
times of steel. What is my staple, it is this, and then some.

A hollering, and then the night-time sky. There is a laugh
Mallarme, that we just cannot shake. And then, when we
dance, we dance for the road, and all she will take.

MALLARME

The holding on we do, and then the release. It is palpable
that we should stand like this. And then, when the sea will no
longer have us, debate, and the measure of sand on glass.

Mallarme, do you see the way? Do you encounter things
unknown? Do you feel, when there is nothing left to feel?
There is a new way to be, that much I know. Yes a new way.

That which should not be, is here. That which is the only
way, is here. That which the dust does not settle, is here.
We have fought long and hard for the right, and now, let us.

Considering the time it takes, there really is little effort to it.
And now, when the noisome brigade have unhinged
themselves – heart and soul, yes, heart and soul. What else.

The light that gives peace to so many is near. The light that
heralds a new turning will come and then, never be seen
again. Cause for celebrating, perhaps; – not perhaps, yes!

A further aside, and then asunder – trees travel further than
we expect. There will be more than the dawn can see. But
can the dawn see? It a further question to ask – how far?

There was a beginning to all this, this is I know. It was not
the beginning I had chosen. But that is okay. We now must
see it through – all the way, and back again. Yes.

Mallarme, do you start to wonder at it all? Are you the one to
see which way to go, in this land of a thousand dreams?
There is a rule here, we must not work it out, or shame upon
us.

A caustic way to show your love. That is why no errands are best. That is why the shape of it is always here. That is why no barriers exist, and no tension allows the bugle.

Running for time, there is a new sense to carry the old. What have we thought, but everything from the beginning. There is Mallarme a wonder to it all, that never leaves.

Hand in hand, heart in heart, this is a way to live. But what is better, is not knowing all-together. And then, in a magic turn of events, a new passion, and a new grace. And then.

Mallarme, do you see the way I have discovered? It is a mist covered lake in the midst of morning. The dawn comes, and sheds its light on the surrounds. And then, magic.

Challenging the Afternoon of a faun. What are we challenging? I haven't known since the dawn of time. But what is it that we seek, in times of grief and yearning? We do not know.

Catching the shards as they fall. This much we can do. This much we can ride upon until we are free. Mallarme, are you the one to swim to abandoned shores, and there, have your fill.

Clutching and clawing. Clawing and clutching. There is a form of silk that doesn't know its length, and that is why we must always be in touch with life itself. This much is true.

Forever bouncing through the hills, never catching a glimpse of the valley's until we are there. We are through now. Mallarme come with us, there is time to be, and time to be still.

MALLARME

Foraging for goodness knows what. We will take our
harvest, and know it to be sure. What is more gripping
though, is that the vine offers a fruit more potent fresh.
Potent for life that is.

Mallarme, are you the starlit, and the grand? Have you no
life to live but the firestorm and the river? Bear in mind, there
will be a new sense of what to foretell. Yes.

There are chances to right the sea as she falls in rapid time
to the chosen beat. And now, where we live that one step
closer, and feeling like the sun will not have us. It is like this.

Mallarme, can you spell destiny, and write it on your hand in
ink? That much we have the feeling for. That much we can
sense of the treacle of life. Do come, I ask of it.

And now, I am the one to not be in the middle of things. I am
one to be on the outside path. Do not deride the soul who
partakes of sand and ancient rhythm. It is hers.

Having said before, Mallarme, what it is that we all seek, we
now must not linger by the stone of circumference, we must
only be entrenched in shards of tomorrow. Be the one.

What has caused us to fall? What has caused us to light the
light, and carry on as if nothing had happened? There is a
place, amongst no places, a place that we come to again
and again. Yes.

Mallarme, falling so close to the edge, it is not a time for
hijinks. There can only be the rounding of winter shores that

contain the air we need to breathe. And then, my Mallarme, and then.

There comes a time, that is not of this earth. It is the way of this earth, but not of it. And then, when we sense its arrival, we can shout in fits and joys, and then partake again.

The ringing true of the forest, Mallarme. This much, at least, is true. And then it comes, the way forward, as we knew it would. We must wait no longer, and then, have our fill.

A blessing, or a curse? There can be in the opposite direction, a new found hearth. And then, when we seek ourselves anew, there is a water that heals. This much we must say.

Mallarme, is the tree twisted enough? Is the family of clouds now as it ought to be? There are times in amongst it, when the scarring of winter nights must not be left with us.

We work hard at our day. We have the feeling like it will never end. But what is closer to the truth, is that it ends, and then continues. This much can be endured, yes.

Opening up to the seam of things. We must believe in something, and this is as good as anything. There are chances that miss, and there are chances that hit. Which one do we want?

The things that bind, are not always the things which ensnare. Mallarme, do you want to know what to do next? All we do is run – run for the hills, and have them fly. Yes.

MALLARME

What we know, and what we don't know, is all about respect.
Respect of the word, and all that is entailed. And when we
hear ourselves anew, a new time, and a new place.

Mallarme, is this you? Is this the man that wanders on moors
mist covered? We have not seen you in a decade, what
have you been ensconced in? Please, by and by, tell us!

There is a chance the wind will only blow from the south
today. And what greater news do we have? Winter is here,
with a cold southerly. This much we approve of, can you
tell?

A solstice that only rights wrongs. What is left behind, will
not answer. What the apparel brings with it. Can we see past
the hedge to see the river cutting through the valley.

Mallarme, there can only be the time it takes to believe once
again that the seeds we sow today, will be the oaks of the
meadow – one day, one day. Hold on, hold on, we have to
see.

Seeing in the mass of it, we come across a new found belief
in things. What we thought was our longing, is nothing other
than our yearning – our yearning to temper what we find.

Mallarme, are you surprised at the candour of it all? Do you
seek respite in the way we have chosen? Be a little bit of
respite, amongst all that you see, and yours will be the
conquered land.

There are times amongst it, that we will never forget. There
are times amongst it, that we will forget, and gladly. But what
of the multifarious display? Do we argue here?

Mallarme, do you see what lies ahead? Do you hear what can only be heard? There is no nicer way, to feel what life has in store. Be the thing that laughs, and the laughter will hit its mark.

What have we sought, but the river? What have we known, but the juniper in sight of spring. There are times to stay, and times to go. And both those times are now. We must not shirk.

Mallarme, the wind, as it comes, it comes in fits and spurts. But its strength is one of the mountain crag, which does not provide shelter. There can only be one way, and that is up.

What is there to say? What is there to do? Can we find the way – it is hidden? We are strong enough to sense things upon us, and have at our beck and call all that is, and all that will be.

Mallarme, what do we have that will take us there? We have the raft of Medusa for us to sail on. We have the pounds of wrinkling shores. We have all that, and more. We will arrive.

The test of things, is in the shallows, is in the water. If it remains calm, we remain calm. There is always some ripple or other, and sometimes a large stone's throw. But that will not keep us.

Mallarme, the stars that have no shape. The stars that have only shape. What we have found in our wandering is more than the twin destinies. What is left to find? Nothing.

MALLARME

What the sands of time have given to the hour. What you and I have found in amongst the rubble. And as in time, so in love. Sport, and the gladdening of things untold.

Mallarme, do you see things clearly? Do you know when to go? Are you a finder after things? In this, there is truth – and a little respite. What do we find when the stars are upon us?

There is a chance, we have, to be what we want to be. There is a chance that we can make ourselves into the whole we want. There is nothing like this in the sky, I tell you.

There was once a dreaming that had as its call the register of the wind. Mallarme, are you the one to give directions to the chalice of delight? Do you see who you are? And then some.

What can never be in the thread of it. What can always be in the womb of it. There is a nicety that bespeaks the untold. And then when the march is over a time to rest, and a time to think.

What is this thing, Mallarme, that straddles the divide? What is this thing that hunts as it forewarns? There are nuances to the tribal will, that only believe themselves to be true.

Aforementioned, and nearing completion. There is never a thing to say, when saying has the barbs of a warm July wind, ringing in the quarters of its completeness. Be still, it will suit.

There is only one place to look, for all that needs looking for. Mallarme, do you fathom the wondering of it all? Do you see what cannot be seen? There is more, that is truth.

What can never be believed, and always foretold. There is a place amongst the embers that glows as solid rocks in tender night. There is a failure in one half, but the other will take us there.

Never before seen. Always feeling the draft. Never seeing what is before us, and only then tripping as if by sight. There can never be what was once there. There can only be this.

Mallarme, a sweet smell. It is the smell of ovens in winter. It is the smell of timings made aright. It is not something we can see in this dark, but our sense of smell will carry us.

A sound I cannot see. Windows in the castle, a whole lot of goings on down below. There can never be a sight so ravishing as this. Be the sea, and its spray will cover us all.

A righteous abandon, Mallarme. Do you see the concubine laden with salt? Is there more to see than what has left the arbour. Catching something through the window. What?

A listening we all do to stave off time. The sense we have to right the ship. The belief we have to see things again. And then, when we least expect, a salve, and an ointment to match.

Mallarme, can you recognise the bitterness in the fruit? Is it there for you as for us? There can only be one rejoinder. The bitterness is there because of the taste we have.

Something worth having. Something worth doing. Something worth the ride to get there. Something worth the bastion that surrounds it. Something for all of us, and all of us still.

MALLARME

Mallarme, do you once again hide from us? Do you see yourself in the mirror in tenfold mass. What is that which keeps us, keeps us going? All the more reason to see again, Mallarme.

A never felt tremor. For tremors, there is no worse fate. But each one of us makes a tremor, and each tremor of us, is felt by others. There can be no greater proclivity than this.

Mallarme, assail the divide that separates you from me, us from the whole. Mallarme, give your wound to the sea, and let it be healed. Give your song to the day, I implore.

Facing north, I head up the road, and then back down again. Nowhere is the same, nowhere is different. There is just talons of the past, and signatures of the future. We will rest.

Mallarme, do you steam in motion through the hills? Do you have what the clouds have? Do you mean what the dawn declares as well? These questions, and more, will placate us.

Separate, and yet joined, the trees of a forest need no reminding, that life is a reminder, and the drenches of autumn rain are here, but only in the midst of this thing we call desire.

Holding on to things, with great gusto – great bravado – great intensity. Holding on things, without care nor favour, nor delight of any kind. There will always be a way. Always.

Each look at the sundial, leaves us lounging to one side, and then up, and around and through and around again. Mallarme, do you hear that sound, it is of us as we shout?

Mallarme, do the sounds of your hearth comfort you? Do the whetstones on the way bring a fire to your soul, and a strength to your steel? Never give in Mallarme, never give in.

The festivities are a light. The things we do to pave the way, are all the more important to those who come after us. So do not tire, do not tire of your way. It will be found.

Mallarme, never have I seen such a performance! The twists, the tails, the turns, that utmost precision of acrobatic nous. There will be more, if we come to the twists with more of the joy.

Have your eyes not seen the way forward, through and back? Have you not witnessed what can never be enough? The time, it is where we will be in the past, present and future.

Mallarme, dream your dream, and come out with nothing left, but the clothes on you. Be all the more ready, all the more in tune with the sea, and what will be then, will be nothing short of all.

Settle yourself, to due duty, and the fanfare which follows in train will be there tomorrow. Have the resting of the day as a sign for play. Have all, and see which is which.

Mallarme, a great lark follows the best, and worst of the day. And here, where a solipsist once read a word, there is no difficulty to remember the words which now come.

MALLARME

Sorrowful, and in touch with all that is. Be my God-send, and we will have a merry time. Be the one who laughs last, and this will be your tournament. Sorrowful, and in touch.

Mallarme, there comes a wistful longing. It does not know where to stop. It only leavers on cankers in the night. There are things we must do, oh companion, things we must do.

The gist of the song rises above the valley, like a mighty incumbency. Be the weather to this song, and the broken lute will have no recourse to the day or the daylight.

I have never known things to be so still. Mallarme, there are times that hark only once, there are times. Be a still mouse in an abandoned abbey. Hear the sound of the dawn's light spilling through the stained glass.

Where were you, my dear soldier, my friend, Mallarme, when the clock struck twelve, and the time it takes to fill a parcel did not litter the ground like a wandering tune. Be that, yes.

Mallarme, have you not seen the latest pictures in the salon? They are truly superb, and done with impeccable taste. Not a pastiche in sight. Thank you, my friend, we have just begun.

The relish we take with us is not of this world. It is of the next, and the brightest, and the most co-mingled. Set up this pace, and you will not feel a thing. Set the world alight, I ask.

There remains a tempest that blows horrid tasks, and sees not the damage of its way. And here, where there are two rungs to climb, the greater and the lesser, we will not hide.

The viscount has a lovely way. And the ardour of the chase
leaves no stone remedied. When we feel ourselves alone, all
we must do, is call on our inner reserves, and enter the fray.

Mallarme, the things we do to dismantle the bridge, are long
and intrepid. Have the never-before-seen way of it come
with us. There are things which should not be, and things
that are.

Wistful, and in need of care, there is never enough of the
rest that cannot come down to beg the rites of passage. In
the middle of it we will learn how to swim, and how to be.

Mallarme, there comes a mighty stasis, that does not find
itself enamoured. In the freedom of the embrace, a mighty
stallion. What is more, something that cannot be reneged.

The place we live in, is in the lap of the sky, and knows no
boundaries. And then, a harlequin mist that hollers stoically,
in the light of the never-knowing. Be with the trees.

What is it here that sends us to the shore, and back again?
Mallarme, there are things to do to explain this, but what of
the night, and all she brings? Not enough of this or that.

What do we say, when to say anything is to cast a vat into
the mire? We sing aloud, like never before, and know that
the best of us is here to be with us, and never to leave.

Mallarme, can you see the mist covered lake? It is for you,
and all you have done. We have never known a moments
rest, but here, the clouds do not part, they only stay.

MALLARME

Falling, but by degrees. A truce enters the fray, and what was fought for, is now salvaged. But the sight of the land all covered in dust is enough to send even the strongest home.

Mallarme, dust-to-dust, the mantel piece beckons you, and sends you humming. What has been the touch stone for so much, is now for the ages. Come, and sing, we are ready.

The very thing we are here to do will send the troupe to the desert shore. And here where we have not found ourselves in many a long year, there will be release, and reconquered land.

Mallarme, the times will not change us – they are us. And then, when the moonlight and the starlight come in shows of strength, a time for peace, and harmony, and all that will be.

The taste we have for the grain, is not of this beseeching wool. And then in the middle of our meal, a full start of classicism to entertain, and keep us going. There it is.

Mallarme, a feasting, and the rye. Have you come for the harvest of humanity? Have you seen the tethered yoke? The song is still with us, and the hills are still in want. Be careful says the leader.

Catching on the turn of it, catching on the seam of things, there is a place amongst all places. The auburn hair is enough to delight. What is more, there can be no more, of this or that.

Mallarme, a cloud to rectify what has gone on. A silence that does not lull. I write for you, here, Mallarme, and know your sound to be one of joy and outpouring. Be content.

The distance between this and that is not our distance, Mallarme. It is the distance of the tempting mire. It is the distance of the fish to men. It is where we do not come in spades.

The senseless abandon that enthrals a kindling stave, is not of the turn of speed that halls a nation state. There is a motion here that cannot be defined, nor travelled with in any direction

Mallarme, can you see once again? Can you see the template for the rising? Is there nothing there to see? The tempest does not surround you, as it does us? Come, we will come.

And then like a fire out of the ash, new breath, and new envisaged steel. There is a long mire that does not wait. There is a tender field, that only embarks. Nothing more can be said.

Appetising and not lacking. We will make it, I am sure, make it to the shore, and then, when we have seen all that is to be seen, a weather on the coast will push us inland – but we will push on.

Mallarme, the time cannot pass us. The sense cannot believe us. The things we shout for are not ours to shout for. And then, when we know for sure, timing and a little silk.

We reach, but for what? We line the things we do with sand, but does it help us? We can come and go, but what does the mist say? There is never a time like now to say, yes we will.

MALLARME

Mallarme, we bridge the gap of the solstice in waiting, but what can our lives tell of, that has not already been said? We linger nightly by the lamp, the lamp that illuminates and settles.

What have we to say now? Is there more in store for the siblings that have no quarter to give, nor semblance to overcome? There is a test in the snow, that rattles and pips.

All that is with us, my dear Mallarme, is all that can be salvaged through time itself. The further we walk, the further the springs are tightened to their effect. Do not simply be, but be more.

Holding on to the rain like we never were, there is a chance to be the things that move in unison of the above. Never strike me until it is time, and then, do your best. Yes.

The feeling I have for the dawn is not one that should be doted upon, but lived to the hilt. Mallarme, is this your feeling to? Is this the one you keep to yourself, and never write about?

The sense of the trees is not our sense. The sense of the rocks is not our sense. We have a milling point to tumble after. And here, where jade is dissolved, more than the recess of things.

Mallarme, I can see the furrow on your brow – was it your growing celebrity, that made you so busy. Was it all the more in tune with things unconquered, and things waylaid.

Foraging through the temporality of it all, there comes a window, out which we can see the sea. You had your

Valvins, Mallarme, and it was your retreat from it all for so long.

There are things nestled in close to the heart, that we never expect to see. But we do, now on occasion, indeed, see them. They are like the window to the heart, that has its chalk in dust.

The test is something of the offering, that has no need to send itself further from our shore, and further from life. In the interim a great cry, that lavishes time itself on to the roof of things.

Mallarme, I have heard it said you were a migrant to these shores, but this is not enough to keep us. There are things that have no flack to believe in. Come, we must away.

These things we see with our eyes, are nothing other than the fruit from the tree, and all its undertaking. The sense the moisture has to see things aright, when its turn comes.

There is a trembling in the seeds of time, that no fought for age had ever had dreams to spill. Mallarme, do you spring in utmost unity, with all that life can give? This is the further shore.

The light is not something that shines on us alone. The lone divagation, is enough to wind the spots down from the roof. And here, where the wounds are near at hand, something that persists.

Catching onto something great. You Mallarme are the belief, the being whose dance is of ice and clay, whose wind is of the twilight, and of the substance that heralds. So come, the time is right.

MALLARME

And then, without care, the nestling of fireflies in darkest night will light up the pitch, and see it to be a renegade with no other bearings. There are stars where the birds used to be.

Mallarme, as if by magic, the weight has lifted, the sand has shifted, and the night-time has held sway. What is more, there is a tune that cannot be sung, for anybody, or anyone.

The seeming impossibility of love. There is more to it than that, of course. But that is the seam of it. There can be no love here, no joy in extant breathing, gazing into the eyes of the other.

Mallarme, there are silken shores that do not waver. There are chances in every wind. They blow when the trees are cut, and dance when the time and chance are right. To it.

Sounds of longing, mists that do not entail. A sense that, at the winning post, there is a parlance that speaks of no other thing, no other thing than that which has been done.

Mallarme, are you a heralding that does not waylay? Are you the one who does not curb it all? Are you the one to fight for hope, passion, and forbearance? This we hope for.

Singing of the night. Sitting in the stream. There was once a solemn mass, that had no music to entail. What we give, is nothing other than the side of things, as they steel to what is next.

Forests, Mallarme, that do not hide. The rustling of feathers in autumn twilight. There is nothing other than these things, as we cross over unto life, unto the day and all she entails.

Gaining in momentum, the slice of life that has us move forward is nothing other than the time it takes to burrow a hill, and lift it skyward, into the air, and back down again, and through.

Mallarme, what is never in our plans, is enough to stall the might of lounging and longing that has as its tail the hope and glass of an age. Never seen like this – yes, and then some.

There is more to this than a feather has rounded out to show. There is a type of composure that none can demolish, and it is in the way we walk, as much as anything.

Mallarme, direct with ease. Direct with calmness and composure, and all that will come to pass will pass through you. This is no telling at the well, but at the coalface itself.

Working to salvage what is going through. There is a chance to estimate the stars for their worth. And when we have nowhere else to go, we catch sight of things as never before.

Mallarme, what is at ebb, is not at flow. There is a possibility that the clouds will only bring rain. But my guess is that they will also bring beauty – the beauty of the dusk, yes.

Bringing in the roses, fostering the tea. What is left of us now we have gone? What is the semblance of things, now that the wholesome food is all eaten? Nothing will compare.

MALLARME

All the milk, my Mallarme, has not had time to ride the sustaining force of life. What we need is for the sun to shine one more time, between this abyss and the next. Come, we will follow.

Happenstance, and the rings of sorrow. What is never more believed, is something that has not the time to stay and fight the fight of tomorrow. Come for the clime, it will suit.

Never in a dream so wild as this, does the same thing arise again, to beat a nearing boon. There can always be time to stay, in twilight, as in noon. But were we there to see?

Mallarme, where is the time? Is it in keeping? Is it is the same space as the rind of life? There are many ways to proceed, but none as perspectival as this. We must come.

Mallarme, a fence to sit on, a joy to ride the voice of indifference. No, there is more here than this. There is more to the tales that we bind in never feeling the way through.

This is where we love to act. Where the shallows are not so shallow, where the times are not so timely. And here where the consternation of deliverance binds, a new fellowship.

Mallarme, you are the tree top, but where are the trees? Have they been cut for last use? Have they been envisaged for the mantle and the pine. No more visage, this is it.

Never hearing things with much the same tutelage. There comes a consternation, to delve right into things, to be the sign post of the day, to be in front, and not behind. To be it.

Mallarme, are you cold? Are you in the cold, and cannot step in? There are never any signs that swing the castle, never any eloping that feels the belief. We will move forward.

The hoping of the mass. What was here, is not there. What is there is not here. There can only be one result, from the starling and the hop, and that is new voice and older muse.

Mallarme, are you one with the reed? Are you stepping on choral made for looking? There can only be the diameter to fold here. There can only be the sense for the moment.

Tremulous, and yet divine. The works in this gallery may even eclipse your Manet's, Mallarme. There are places that are wondering in lost eclipse. Be the monument, be the train.

Mallarme, see the random shouts, see what is not coming out. And here, where the noise is in stationary formation, a vocalising of the need of the dearest apprentices. Be here.

Coining a new phrase. Coining that which cannot be coined. Live for the ages, live for the sea, live for anything, but do not miss the show. It is of the lifetime, and can only be once.

Mallarme, the sights for your eyes. The sights for your deeds. The sights, and then some. We forage in amongst it, and know the sand to be a troubadour. Be a blessing, it will help.

Forsooth, and all that is. What we come for is the semblance of normalcy, one that doesn't shy from the day, or from the whispering of night in grains and sand. Be there.

MALLARME

Mallarme, have the pyramid of your choosing, but do not linger, there is a time for festivities, but they are not now. There can only be one thing to eventuate, and we must let it unfold.

The only thing to do, is run and hide. No, never, we will fight with not an ounce of reluctance. We will gather the clouds, so that they can be gathered no more. Once, and then?

Mallarme, wishing for sand. Wishing to have the sand run over his hand. There is never anything more than this. There is never anything more, nor anything less, less than this.

A culture, in the weave of it. It is needed to overcome the best of life. And here where we do not fend, a fecundity that has only bite. There is more than sand here, much more.

And when it comes, Mallarme, a new time to dance – to dance in the way of it. We have never seen such movement, lead on, sweet Mallarme, lead on to the troupe that has no meter.

Falcons that tear down walls, with each passing beat of an eager thumb. There is never a cry for help, and here, where we linger, a feeling like the trace had come, and never looked back.

Mallarme, seeing the tension in the wings, of birds that do not fly. There is a new sense of old wounds, and a salient heart. Come, we will not pass the time, we will only shout.

A grand hooray for all that is. What is left, cannot call to arms. What is left does not have the motion of things. We see without intent, the lands of faraway people. Yes, be strong.

Mallarme, are you with us, or against us? Are you in the
wind, or without the mire? Do we sing in times of drought,
that holds its feet in magnificent spires? Come now, we
must away.

Washing up the density of it all, we find ourselves once
again with no light to shine, nor no figure of speech to be
had. But there is life, and where there is life, there is this.

Mallarme, a song and a dance, and washing of fables of the
night. What can never be lost, is always found. And here,
where we sing so timely, a sort of sleep that knows no rest.

A foraging that finds it all. A newness that lands a great
distance. Without the sound of time to guide us, are we even
here? Do the sounds of yore beat a mighty heart, and then…

Mallarme, sounds of longing, and a solemn march. These
are the things that binds us, tether us, and then let us go.
What we see when we open the door is enough to startle.

Having a forward motion. Delving in deep. What is never for
the forging, is always for the curse. Be the test of a
dandelion, and yours will be the sound. What never fails, is
this.

Mallarme, have you heard the cry, the cry of the night? Have
you loved, loved the sky at daybreak? Have you been the
summer in the depths of winter? Have you been forlorn?

The wrestling of autumn leaves. There is nothing like the
time of it, this time of year. There can only be one outcome,

MALLARME

and that is the carry the elder bush through bleak times. Yes.

Mallarme, you have something, we don't, and that is knowledge of the after-now. Yes, it is a mighty thing. You know with absolute certainty. And for that you must be thankful.

Gaining in motion, the speed of it harangues the stallion itself. But before we let go completely, another chance at what can never be lost. There is movement where there should be stillness.

Mallarme, we long to see your dance. Your favourite movements from a time no longer ours. But that is okay, don't you think? To let some energy into the room, and then, flood.

The silence is overwhelming. Just a little at first, and then like a diatribe in thin air. There is motion too. At first slow, then fast, then slow again. What is it that tempts us so?

Mallarme, your wings are cast in bronze – why is it that only bronze wings can fly? There is never enough to see properly here. But that is okay, we will fathom the walk.

A tutelage that reminds us of the time we had before all this began. What is the sound of spinning forks doing here? That is fine, we will carry them forward into night.

A whole host of togetherness. There is never a break in the road that will let us in. Come now, there are forces at play here, we cannot comprehend. For one more time.

Mallarme, do you harbour the ghost of a thousand
ablutions? Is this your parting grace? Can the sands that
carry you, carry you forward, and not backwards? And then.

Burying objects in the sand hoping they will be found by
future generations. Your sand is full, Mallarme, and people
are finding it's objects. Yes, and when we are through,
togetherness.

There was once a saying, that said, 'Oft to the many, to the
many, Shangri-La, Shangri-La'. And then, in the midst of it, a
new type of saying; 'Shangri-La to stay, to stay'.

Mallarme, in the time of crises. There is never enough of
anything to placate the artists and the playwrights. But we
will be forward in our backwards motion. We cannot do
otherwise.

What was not buried in time to our chosen piece. There is a
signed way below the turn, that catches onto all that bites.
And here where we run that new mile, a chosen piece, once
again.

Mallarme, is yours of the apple, and the sound of claps? The
district is in need of further turns, and greater than this, in
need of games to play. Will you come forward to see?

Often, we say, 'down to the bottom, up to the top'. But
otherwise, there is no life. You don't peak too soon, nor feel
sorry for your life, and there can be an outcome, that doesn't
hark.

Mallarme, you and me, and all that can make it. Come for
the rigour, and be a part of the adventure. Come down and

MALLARME

send the merriment through the in-between of things once again.

And so, in the meaning, and the diatribe, there exists the wanton harshness of the lascivious nature, as it turns once again to the life of it, and knows not which way to go.

Catching a hold, Mallarme, catching a hold of the thoroughness of things. There cannot be a trade in the sparkle of it all, no thing to hark back to, no rhyme to listen to.

A vestige of things to come. Why do we not come for the season, when the season is nothing other than the orc of our malcontent? There is a faith in it, I guess. There is time.

Mallarme - we have sparked a thing that does not rival a companion to staple by. There are movements in the heavens that have no longer any gait. We have been on land too long.

And then, when we are least aware, a sizeable acquaintance who never knows where to be, and where not to be. Further from the truth, we are now in line with the stars.

Mallarme, dearest of the dear. Come for the ardour of it all. Come for what is next. Come for the chance to breathe once again, one last breath. And here, a semblance to admire.

A forest clearing, charmed in light. A never ending waterfall, that simply does not know how to stop. A weather that makes all things possible. There will come a time. Yes.

Paul Fearne

Mallarme, are you there, beneath the laden cloth? Are you in the middle of something deeper? Do hands of chosen silk not belittle you any further? You must come!

In our hands there is something more. There is sand, but there is also something more. What is it? What is it that we seek? The sand falls, but what of life? Never a backward step.

Mallarme, we see you coming – hooray. We see the sky open, and then you, in all your finery. What is left of your time, is not of this page. What of your time, what of your time?

Indifferent to the water that takes us there, I lull back again into winter harbours. There is nothing but waiting here, but that is okay, for wands of the far and near will accompany us.

Mallarme, a sight too far. A need too strong, a feeling of the never, the never as she rushes to lands untold. There is something like this everywhere, everywhere as we carry on.

Holding the lamp, as it tumbles down. Being in touch with so much. There are tingles down my spine, there are hearsays that do not bend. We will find you in the in-between of times.

Mallarme, have you forgotten? Have you forgotten the saying you once had? What was it? What was that saying? 'Never besides the strength of it'. We will come, and we will know.

Having a ritual in place, having the sand in the hour glass. There are monstrosities here, but maybe Poe has placed them – with quill of steel, and arch of bent light. Yes.

MALLARME

Mallarme, does the saying follow us? Do we have reverberation down spines unbent? There is a line in the sand here, a line that must not move. What of it – we will see.

Guarding the natural light, there comes a splendour to things unknown. What have we fought for, but all that is? What have we come to, but lines unbent? Come with us, please.

Mallarme, you don't seem to like the intransigence of things. What is more, you don't seem to see the way down the hill. Have no fear, dear man, we will catch the next invective.

Forests that do not grow. Ablutions that are not hurried. What we lack is nothing short of all. What we come for, is nothing in the way. Be the bliss, and I will be your reminiscing.

Mallarme, is it true? Do you languish on a heap unknown? Do you have what is left, and then no more? There are things we must not see, and this is one of them. Do you see?

Having the courage to feel that one last time. Being in the midst of it, only for the fun of it. What we say is never enough. What we say, can only be the thing that is enough.

Mallarme, do you ricochet with abandon, when it is your turn? Can we see your dance before it is too late? What is the stallion you have there – does he gallop at speed's unknown?

A gaining in momentum. A lark before the day. There is nothing to do here but set wheels in motion. But what motion is this? What commotion? We will see, and then speak directly.

Mallarme, has the wind forsaken you? No – only the breeze has taken up a shallow falter. What can be said otherwise? There is nothing left to be by. No, there is only all.

Having something to say, and not saying it. Having the drenching rain come again. Having the soul to mend what we need. There is a moisture that does not dry, and only wells again.

Mallarme, the chains that bind, are the same as the shards that are want to bury deep. We can only see ourselves in the mirror, and here things are like mesh, and do not stale.

Giving more, to take less. What we say, when the night-time invigorates, is like the ocean at full capacity. There is a tale here, that knows no dimension, nor salt of truth. Yes.

Mallarme, a round spinning thing, that turns no tables. And here, where we have found ourselves again, we will nod in vague nonchalance at the moon, and see it to be a ghost no longer.

Shifting onto the sands of temperance, a new found need, harks back to where it all began. And here, where temperance is a thing well known, a frost will bend its hoary feather.

Mallarme, there comes a time, when we must listen to the waves, and let their sound navigate our ship, as we come

MALLARME

tumbling down. This is what life is for, for the taking of chances, and chanceless oars.

There is something here. There is something that beats upon these shores. And then when we are through, a nice feeling that rises and falls as the day. Be lost in it, it will not vary.

Mallarme, a long rest, and then, back to work. We must work, and feeling so, we harvest dreams as we harvest sunsets – in wonder and in awe. Be the thing that makes us.

Having a wander through life's square. The fruit is for sale here, and all that is left of the day is in the night's escapade. Can we see again under the canopy of night – I think so.

Mallarme, do we dare? Do we dare move forward through ages of ice, ages of brick? There can be nothing more to say here – nothing more in the repertoire. Let us go and see.

Finding fate as she bends over another shoulder, and then back again. There is never a thing that willows in times of great abandon. There is always something left, and then left again.

Mallarme, my companion, shoulder your arms, give sustenance to the weary. Be a blight, but not a weave. Be in tune, but not with all. Have the noise call itself back, and you will win.

What have we believed in, that has not come to pass? What have we seen in the rubble but faces of drawn out silk? There will come a change, that has no difference in its heart.

Having the wedding during the day, and seeing all your friends during the night. We love what is best, and not what is worst. Does this make sense my Mallarme – does it?

Bliss and tumbling – hurtling over tree top. There can only be what is left. And here where we see again in crimson steel, a light weight of candour enters the fray, and says, 'Indeed'.

Mallarme, an inch below the scar. And here where we love the most, most things do only happen in halves. Running at random speeds, we face the day, and then have our say.

Forced into an alcove, we see our lives drift in dreams of dew covered grass. And here, an amazing aperture, one that does not blink in time. Do we see the colours anew?

Mallarme, away, and through, and in sense with, and then, once again, and through, but not in half. We will come again before the mist is away, and then over, and about.

Catching up with the pejorative, I find the superlative, and know that crescent moons have their sense too. There can never be anything more than this, anything more than the tide.

Mallarme, do you belie your fate? Do you cast about for dreams in phantom waters? Is this what the marrow is like? Can we be that far and away? These are questions, but what are the answers.

Much is said in the twilight, and much unsaid. But when the rain banishes down on solemn rituals, there comes a chase that has not the heart to let go. But we must, we must let go.

MALLARME

Mallarme, you see now, like you have never seen before.
We know the gate to be open, and so we swing far and
wide, through, up and beyond. There can never be anything
other than this.

Wishing that the tide should not come. Hoping that the fence
we sit on will not break. And here, where we love to be,
there are a dozen things to do, but we have not done them.

Mallarme, find yourself again, and steam forward like an air
hole in the summer. Do not renege your bastion, there will
be time to catch all reels, and to know them for the first time.

Finding wrath, the wrath of the undiluted. There are times we
cannot remember, and times that do not stay. But when we
are through, a solemn rite, one towards which there is
nothing else.

Mallarme, are you gaining in dimension, or is it the wind that
hollers at your door? I will give you the grinding stone, so
that you might fashion a ring, that will have you for the ages.

First and foremost, yes, that is the one we seek. First, and
yet last, syncopated and in dreaming, there is nothing we
can find without the trail in our eyes. This much is true.

Coming and going, my Mallarme. Coming and going,
through reams of tethered silk. Do not shine on the day like
a ferryman out for a night-time stroll. There will come time
for more.

Mallarme, since you are here, let me say there can never be
time to hurry, always time to be slow. There is, in this mist, a
laden fruit, that has no mark, nor kindness to bestow.

Guiding with glue made from a wreck. Guiding with an insatiable appetite. Guiding with the trees as they bend, guiding with all that we see, and more. There will come a new season.

New festivities that gain in time of wonder. There will always be a way. There has always been a way, and there will always be a way. This much we can be sure of in dead of night.

Mallarme, a new song. Mallarme, a sense to the senseless. When we come, we come in oaks made of iron. There is nothing else but the dawn. There is nothing else.

Foreign to these climbs. Without a seed of doubt. With more of the same, and less of the other. We are here to take stock, and then move forward, as if by magic. Come and be a part of it.

When we dance, my Mallarme, when we dance, we dance for you, and that is true. Come, don't stand still, there is much to be done, and much to be undone. Sing in due course. Yes.

A feather that does not know where to tread. A knowing smile, from one lover to the other. A sort of kindness that does hold back. What we thought was the end, is only the beginning.

Foraging, Mallarme, foraging for something difficult. Always resting upon, never reclining outright. Be that as it may, a sound that can placate, and hear itself anew. Yes.

MALLARME

There was once a time to be, to be like no other. And now, just as the right and the solemn descend from the heights, there is a negligible impact, that soars like no other.

Mallarme, is this the way? Is this the way forward through illimitable wastelands? Is this what we have come to see? Be a feather in an urban mass, and the breeze will blow for you.

Further than ever before, we are filled with life, and the water overflows from the font. Do what we know is right, and the daylight will savour a new type of soul, one that weeps only in joy.

Mallarme, something that links us to the stars. Something that we treasure, and something that the night cannot belittle. There are things we do not understand, but that is okay.

Bringing forward the round, so that we can be in the middle of something greater. Whispering footsteps on frost covered ground. Harbouring long lost feelings as they scatter full length.

Mallarme, you once put out a journal, that lasted eight editions. Upon its folding, you were left in a state of pecuniary distress, like you were warned it would. But that is okay, all for literature.

Linking up to the saddle, so that we might rain again, on treasures made of wood, treasures made of sand. The little bit we see of the road, is enough to fill us with dread.

Mallarme, what is better left unsaid, is here in full union. The
distress we feel at life is not of this land, is not of this sea.
The welling up of chests unhindered, is now a victory in full.

Mallarme, a mighty holler, a magnificent bravado. Where the
stars do not signal, and the rain does not fall, there is a
space between double rainbows that lets dreams in, and
never out.

Gaining in strong strides, the last of our known vestiges
comes for the ride. We carry it in lasting spread, and see the
same of other years as they bend again in unison and light.

A watchful scene, that harbours untold feelings, feelings that
are only here in untold rhymes. The chance to start again,
the chance to be what we thought we never could.

Mallarme, listening to the harp that never was. Listening to
all the signs and signals of the day. And then when we are
through, a place to be still, and be alone, and be calm.

There are things in this world that do not glisten. There are
things in this world that have no pout. And here, where we
find ourselves once again, a new way to be, and be through.

Searching amongst the rubble, Mallarme. There is time here
to wrestle with angels, and give the firmament a glance of
steel, before all is laid at the circumference of things.

Honing wandering thoughts, and fashioning them into new
thoughts, new thoughts for old. A resolution comes, to ease
our weary bones, but this is brief, and only holds the tide for
a short time.

MALLARME

Mallarme, do you see yourself in times of trouble, times of difficulty? This is the founding chaff of an age old quandary. What do we live for? Why stay, when to stay, fights?

Grains of molten lead that do not lead the way. Receptacles of a different sort, that only carry what we need. Have we done the journey to its completion? We will see it through.

Mallarme, a swarming of abandon that only has endearment as a mechanism, something to soothe all wounds, and savour all ties. What is this we seek? Do we have it?

Changing things around, so that we never get left in the cold. Being lost, and then being found – being perturbed, but never wound up. A nervous complaint, nor the time it takes.

Mallarme, a single note at dawn, something to take the sheen of things. There is like nothing else here – there is the wind, the rain, the clouds, the lightning, and the free for all.

More of the time it takes to rumble for the temporal, and all that comes to pass. There is only what we have, and then intransigence, and all that time can see. Yes. Time.

Mallarme, are you the one to say, yes to the storm cloud, as it beckons? I believe you might be the one to laugh at night as she fills gaps of untold delight into maps of shear audacity.

Beginning once again, so that we see each other for the first time, and know the chasm for what it is, a brief dalliance that has no might. No might, to see the way we see.

Mallarme, are you true, are you the sand, and the dune, and the rain, and all that shall be? Be more than we had hoped, and the misery of the sun will not rain down on us ever again.

Jasmine, and all that will follow. There is never, in the wind, a surety that harks back to times of grandiloquence, and then round again, and through, and towards – this much we know.

Mallarme, there is a levity in the wind of things. We are allowed to swallow large portions, but only to satiate our needs. Never look forwards, the sand is there, sand to hide.

Having the test and winning through. Having the most arduous oblivion set aside, and still managing to get there. There is a chance that the noise will not linger, which is fine, indeed.

Mallarme, a sigh, and then through. What we have been given is a mighty vision to see through the dark, and out into the world. But these words are merely a fine adumbration, that harks back to things. We will be vision filled.

Foraging close to the shore, our journey wins a reprieve from the mistletoe above. And then, when we come that little bit closer to the entrance, there will be a mighty cry, and then...

Mallarme, what do you see before yourself? What do you see, in the dark edges of a portent that foretells of hardships and niceties? What is it there that so festoons the scene? Yes.

MALLARME

Fashioning an old piece of wood into a raft. And here where we long to be, there is a passage from an old book which gives us heart. And here, where we laugh the loudest, new beginnings.

Over the foothills of life, over the dale of existence. There is here, my Mallarme, a new turn of speed. The stallion is strong, and we are weak next to it – but we will hold on.

Catching a ride on a carriage that has known a thousand miles. It is here that we see ourselves anew, and here that the sound of longing does not reach us. There will be time.

Mallarme, a saying that awaits. A feeling that does not die. There is a wind in things that never dies. And here, where we have waited so long, a supplement to the wise. Yes.

Having our fill, and seeing life as it is. We will now know ourselves in the thick of it. We will only know ourselves, once we are through, a type of exposure that languishes.

Mallarme, are you the one to come, to come to distant shores – to come to places never before seen, to never before heard of? Come, we must away, then, find ourselves again.

There is in this place a further word. It is the nuance of fate as she comes again in times of steel, times of cascades. Never before has there been such malaise. We are in touch.

Mallarme, are you the one? Are you the one to fill our sails to the up-most point, and then come again for shards of the ready-handed? Do not despise us, we only come for you.

Catching sight of the barge that will take us there. Catching sight of the wind that will charge our vessel. Be the simplest in terms of dimension, and the loadstone will not fail.

Mallarme, the one of kind felicity, that does what it can. And then, without the nearest time, a new found welling that dispenses as it wanders. Can we be the surest of foot? I hope.

Happening like a new sea-scape, like the tail fin of a large fish, like the sense we have to be the trade, and not be the want. There can only be one result. And that is to see.

Mallarme, a sign that we were here. A countenance that lingers slowly. What we felt in the middle of it all. What we grew to love over the years. What we found to heal old wounds.

Which way to go, when the lights are faded, and the time it takes to run a mile is half that which is used to be. There will never be an hour-glass that will be full, this much is true.

Having a new found wish, that doesn't replace the old, but renews things, as if they were not real. The difference in the song to the tailor, is not as much as we might think.

What we have always felt, and never let go of. And here, where the sands are of the parade, there will come a new deliverance, to repartee the old. What a time, what a place.

Mallarme, do you know of the hirsute, in times such as these? There is no time like the willing, like the mire and the tread. What have we found, that is not like more than enough.

MALLARME

Catching hold, on leaves and branches, on dale and round, on simplicity, for simplicities sake. We will shake what it is that holds us back, and then, exemplar and the wind.

Mallarme, do you listen? Do you listen to rival the sounds of a quandary, which has no quarry but the land of snow and ice. There is a way forward, but never a way back. We will come.

When we hear our own voice in the wire, we contort that little bit more. And here, where breathing becomes difficult, a lighter breeze will spring up, to guard the unwary.

Mallarme, do you believe once again, that light will have its way with the dark, and that the way forward will not undo itself in the placating. Come and see this, for the time being.

Never again shall the rain be so indelible. Never again, shall we be that thing that harbours regrets. The moisture here, does not bleed, but only gathers, to round out our souls.

Mallarme, is this the way forward? Is this the way we go? It is as if a levity had sprung up between us, and the wheels to spur us on had become disentangled, and away!

Foraging through things, is like the testament to an unknown trail. And when the load is heaviest, there will come a sound. It will help ease our difficulty, and then, without care – release.

Mallarme, what have you to say? What have you to do? Can you come again in light, as in darkness – can you be who your fellows are not. Gone is the wind – here is the rail.

There is in amongst it a new type of seed. It follows as it unhinges, and bleeds as it goes down. When the harrowing and the need are upright, there is never anything to go by.

Mallarme, do you see what we cannot – are you the one we believe you to be? And in the night you will come, and there will be a mighty fire, enough to let the fathoming want.

Hark, and see, oh hand of mine. Be the one to sense the danger, and do what you can to stop it. There will be nothing more of the manner to speak in tongues of golden thread. Yes.

Mallarme, a fragrant rice allures the destiny of choruses, and in the fiction of togetherness, there is a light as it comes in shades – shades that have no fear, nor want.

Holding on, we see you come, and know you to be a ram for the hedges. Be the maypole and yours will be an inch to the mile. Do not delay, there can be only what is left.

Mallarme, a sense of the shortness of it all. Something we can hang our hats on when the vastness dissipates. And here, where we swing, from this rafter to the next, a sound.

Sounds in the dark. Sounds of something encroaching. There is always the way forward, never the way back. We have seen it here, in the closing of doors. Here and there.

Mallarme, do you swim? Do you fight the water before it drains? Is there enough to see by, see into things, and through, and roughly enough? There will come the change my friends.

MALLARME

When we sink, we float. When we dive, we swallow. And here, where the sound of forever is a distant memory, there can be only what we need to get us to where we want to go.

Mallarme, are you the one to wish for greater things? Are you the one who sees the bastion full? The cup is in the mire. The cup is in the sea. This cup holds all we need, and then some.

A gaining of the rightness of things – doing what you feel you must. Doing all those things that the temperance of the spade tells us we must. And now, we will truly be, and be true.

Mallarme, a song of songs. A new found heartache that does not tell the time. A whisper in the trees that has no sound. A wanting that deserves more, deserves less.

On the whole, things are where they should be. But this doesn't mean pleasantness, or that the right things are happening. It is that things aren't insouciant, and the climb is difficult.

Mallarme, you are a fool – a fool for what? For life, for literature. And then, what is next, the whole, and the harvest. The little bee, and work till twelve. There can be no other way.

What is now, is the rain as it comes. What is now, is the solemnity of an age. What is now, is the wind as she comes from places unknown. Be still, it will suit you, and the times.

Mallarme, the want is the window, the sire is on the hill. Where we the last ones to laugh, and did we laugh best? Did we laugh blest? Did the laughter ring the truest it has?

Coming up for air, there is no sound otherwise. No sound to hear, none to vie with. And when we swing, we swing for all time, and we do it not just for us, but for the many who follow.

Mallarme, are you the one to take us there? Are you the one to sense the light is right, and to come on your stallion from a faraway place, and know it to be true? Please, yes.

A plumb, a nuance, a new found longing. There is everything we believe to be – there is more in fact. And here where we are radiant in colours, a somnolence that does not overcome.

Mallarme, the tried and true – the keepsake and the combustible. And now in clothes made of red, that don't give the back hand demise to the world. There will be time, there will be time.

Fasten on, there is a way to go. There is movement in the hills, there is a time to be waylaid, and answer to the trees in a night-time gale. What do we want from this? What do we need?

Mallarme, quick, come, do not bleed. There is space here for the climb, space here for the deliverance. Space here, oh one, of sharpest of the sharp. Do not be special, be one.

Heaviest of heart – transpiring of togetherness. Can there really be the way home, when the way forward is blocked at every turn, every corner? Yes there can be, and there will be.

Mallarme, do you sing, sing that song, that has never been sung. We are here to sing it, so sing it for you now, we will. OOmpapa Ompappa, hey yeah, hey yeah. That is all!

Never before has the smoke risen above the plains. Never before has that which remains unspoken let such a sigh at the means of deliverance. Be in one with the sky.

Mallarme, do tell of your most recent adventure. Did you lie on beaches untamed? Did you live in dominions unnamed? Did the force of it send you spinning through channels aghast?

Nearing late in the castle, the evening moon casts its pall over the ramparts, and lets fall the might as simple muses. In the night, in the night. In the night, there are plain trees.

Mallarme, there are times to go, and times to stay, and which do you prove along? You stay, of course. That is your want and your invective. Be a treasure then, in your staying.

Hoping to find, all that will settle. Hoping to be, all that will find its way. And then, out of the mist, a chance at rain, and a chance to settle the score. Be a labourer in labourer's garb.

Mallarme be the chosen, and then choose wisely, there will be a letting be at the end of proceedings. Do not hear yourself in the wanton music? Be the time it takes to broach a net.

Marching over hill and dale, there is much to be said here in the intransigence of it all. The message is clear – we must away, before the canyon fills us, fills us with the breath of life.

Mallarme, are you the sun, that shines on so much? Do you stand near the pleasant garden, hoping to see a sight, never to be forgotten? There will be time, my Mallarme.

There is never the sense that lines in sandy shade could encompass that which is in us already. What do we do, to seek the shade we need? We set off without a flinch, and then return.

Mallarme, singing in the way of it. Never hearing, always going, seeming like time will go on forever. Be the mass of it, being the one who whistles at the labyrinth. Come, let us go.

The solidity and the dawn – what is next, and how, round-a-bouts. Be the semblance, and your reward, will be all. Never doubt this, it is written in script. And then some.

Mallarme, time to be, and be intractable. There can be no clouds in the sky fast enough, nor lines through the sand straight enough. And here where we love, a new festivity.

And now, when the reaches of autumn light come in winter, there will be a new sort of wondering – one that will shear the sky of its very plumpness. Do not be afraid, we will come again.

Mallarme, the sun, oh the sun – there is in this bushel a might and cable, and something that can never be. Here, where we wonder through life in endless array, levity, and the ends that meet.

MALLARME

Silence in the pasture, noise upon the hill. There is a tension in the ring of things, that must not be forgotten. Be in the charge of the night, and yours will be here. Come, we must go.

Mallarme, I see your tension as it builds upon your shoulders. Tension, and the ilk of the way. Do not be concerned, my friend, there is only a difference in the way we see things.

Gaining in acceptance, gaining in togetherness. Sounds are a stroke here, that do not harvest a sentence. There is only what will may, and even then, there is the sound that barks.

Mallarme, a new type of adjustment, that relieves the weight of all the time that has elapsed. When we come again, there can be no more of the song, and only of the day.

Feelings of utmost resolve. There is in this movement, a stoic meter that believes in things to be as they are. What do we say now, oh treasure amongst the hive. Be in two halves.

Mallarme, have you seen your destiny in a nutshell? Have you felt the warmth in a package sent from the hereafter? What is this that we say we have? Is it in us to toll the bell?

Questions of punctilious might. Well thought out desires that only have in them the waste that is no more. Love in the arbour, longing in the way. There are sounds here that echo.

Mallarme, do the songs of the daylight argue to the teeth? Do we argue ourselves, without really knowing? Do we find a way that has nothing of the silk and the fibre? Yes, and then?

Gathering to reach the hub. Sounding more like the hearse everyday. Never really being satiated - only in dreams. Gaining in temperance, but not knowing why. There is more still to come.

Mallarme, a whistle, a whistle that makes no sound. There is much to do, and even more to undo. The test of it is in the salt of it. The test of it is in the way we move ourselves, from here to there.

We have never seen this in all our lives. What is it that we have never seen? It is the heart, as it pushes blood. It is the eyes, as they scan the horizon. It is all of this, and more.

Mallarme, do you feel as I do? Do you want the path to be a reckoning, and the fables about its difficulties to be true? Come now, we must not think of such things, only of what is not.

Over, and under - through, and then before. Something calls to us as we sleep, and we don't know it's source, so we come down from our slumber, and follow, and then, start the day again.

Objects in the twilight, sounds around the bend. What we love to do, is to rest weary limbs on tables made for feasting, and then, when we least expect – jump, and up and onto.

Hanging on, in the hope of another stay. Clinging to the shards of it, so that we never will have to ever again. I am loving this, so that I may not have to love another. Beginning through.

MALLARME

Mallarme, sounds that have their fairness about them. Intrepid adventurer, whose lost taming is not of the world. Come, you cannot believe more in things, now and then.

Rest, and be assured, that the time for us is a mighty wand that has no space to breathe, and no lapse to seed. There are times when we wish for otherwise, but that is not now.

Mallarme, the things that send us spiralling, are not the same as the things that find us circling. Be the one, and not the other. Be in the here, but the now? Of course, of course.

Wishing for the tendrils to let go, there is a catch in the seam of things that has no air to rejoice, and no invigorating resplendent to take care of. Do we all feel the same, I hope so.

Mallarme, is yours the good king, who summons all and sundry to his court to go and send the news afar, that life is of the essence, and the thing which binds us all, is life itself.

Further and further, the text travels. To distant shores, and outright paws. There are testings for each aplomb as they go further still, to places of amazing adventure, and back again.

Mallarme, have you sought the news yourself? Is it readable, and in a succinct fashion that knows only itself to tread the vine and the rosary. Be in the middle of things.

Sense, and the way of it. The senseless, and all that it seems. There are things we do not understand, but things we watch in flightless wonder. Do not be afraid, it comes for others.

Mallarme, do you see yourself in the time it takes to fathom the ocean? Do you see what we are when we are awake, a glowing steel that melts the snow in cascading want?

Holding on, there is a theme to this. Holding on, there lies a rhyme too, that does not bleed. Holding on, there is more in the seam of it than the noise it makes going away.

Mallarme, sure in the wind. Sure is the sea. Sure without end, and then, when a saying is enough, enraptured, and all that is pure, and will not sleep. Come and be a part of it!

Running through the hills, and having a sounding board with us. Running through the hills, and being in line with Jupiter. There are posing's that ride no mass. There is the here and now.

Mallarme, laughing, running, being still. Do you have the sand between your toes, the moisture in the air, and sun in the arbour? Do you feel what is not lost, and not forgiven?

Having the bastion, and nearing its hearth. There is now no time left. No time to shut the windows to the sea, no time to tread on ancient shores, no time, and then a glimpse of it.

Mallarme, are you a one to believe in the very fibres of things, to the very core, to the very aperture of respite. Do you come in needs of silver, needs of grey, needs of the unending?

The gnashing and gnawing of fate. The tempest that does not lie in wait. The hallow man who sings as he wakes,

wakes from a deep dream, a deep slumber, only to return to this!

Mallarme, a final farewell. Much that is done, and much that is left undone, there are curiosities here that leave no bounds, and things that we do that leave us lounging and dishing.

All that is here, all that I am, all that is in the way, is here, beside me ready for you, oh air, oh sun, oh moon, oh things which divide, and have yet to conquer. Be worthy, it will suit.

Mallarme, release me from my fate – you cannot – nobody can, but that is okay, I have chosen it, well it chose me, but I accepted! Do not follow suit, there are times to stay.

There, in the mist, there is something more to say. Something more to be said, that overcomes as it launches. Be that thing, and yours will be a never before seen acceptance.

Mallarme, are you the healer of old wounds? Are you the wandering of old fireflies? Do you sleep, and dream of what is next? Do you come for the buoyant mood, and then away?

Is there something that we are pleased to see? Is it in us to see, what we have always thought possible? We are the way of it, as you are the muse. Do not fight, there is no more.

Mallarme, do you saddle up your horse, much like the rain has done in times past? Do you see the roundabout as a toy, or as an instrument of learning? Please be assured.

Paul Fearne

Now that we have stayed that extra time, we will come full circle, and know the last to be first, and the first to be last! Come on our merry way, there is no time like acceptances.

Mallarme, what have you thought that we have not thought, that we have longed to think? Coming in steadily, through a gale, a nuance, and a wing. There will only be what is there.

Something special in the night. Something to feel a light by. There is never anything that we can do here. There is only what is precious, and then the harvest will be finished.

Mallarme, are you the charging horse? Are you the wind as it blows down a thousand makeshift abodes? Be the messenger, I implore you, do not move, there is never a chance.

Come, the room is empty. The sign on the mantle reads much. There can always be a time for lingering regret, regret of the forewarned, and regret of the age. Be the troupe, you will stay.

Mallarme, there are things that do not shine, and there are things that always placate the day. Never before have we seen the vision that is the transformation of everything we have thought dear.

Listing on a sea, so wild that none can take hold of their rafts. The night is a vision, as the truth of it is wandering star. Be the mode of so many, and yours will be the division of labour.

Mallarme, can you see the wings, the wings which will take you there? Can you see what the wisps of wind are doing to the transit of the planets? Can you be the one in a ship of fools?

Having the intent, and seeing it through. Wishing for the harbour, and not quite knowing. What we thought was the day, is nothing but the night. What is left of you and me?

Mallarme, do you hope for it? Do you hope that lines in times of straggling are enough to launch the dawn for one last adventure. One last vine to climb. One last need to be.

And then, when we laugh at things, there is a pleasantness that unhinges as it delights. There is more now than we can conceive. There is a harbour that none know about.

Mallarme, a wisp that knows no longing. A tendril that harbours victory in the light of day. What is there to say? What is there to do? What can we nearly be, as a shadow in moonlight?

Gaining once again the land of our ancestors. Having a rest, until we know we are rested. Being in tune, like the sand between our toes. Never running, always walking.

Mallarme, do you settle for what is best? Do you climb on the backs of angels, until you can climb no more? Is there something you must do, so that your doing will be transcendent?

Looking into the glass, and seeing what is there. Seeing what is there, and demarcating the outline to be a thing of truth. Be in line with the stranger – he will take you far.

Mallarme, do you have the right, the right to write you name in the sky, and have it stay? And when we come, there is a droning that does not envisage all that is – come, we must.

Holding on to things, before they have arrived. Letting things happen, until we reach the end. And then we will find a new envelope, and write on the front 'Literary Estate', and then, the end.

Mallarme – away, and away, and away – yes, we must again. We will find more than a fathom in the depths, let me be clear from the start. But what is marked as sure, will remain so.

There is a time for the nightingale to be as it chooses. There is time for us to be as we chose, there is in us that capacity. But what have we thought, but all that is. What have we been, but similar.

Mallarme – do you see, all that you can, do you feel the night, as it rains in shards of colour, unseen in the dark. Is there more to us, more than the ransom on coasts of yore.

What is this thing for? What are the grooves that make it move? What have we found, but all that is. What have we sung, but every song. There is nothing left for us. Nothing but this.

Mallarme – a new way to be. A might that has no right. A willingness to see things through. A happenstance that does not deteriorate. A bringing forth that has no time to waste.

What have we come for? What have we come for that does not waylay? There is a chance we have, that does not include the way of things. What should we say, that does not foreclose?

Mallarme – what is this thing called fate? What is this thing that causes no pain? What do we do with ourselves, before it is too late? What have we come for, before it is all gone?

Gaining in stature, the right line belittles the comfort we feel. Have you know, that the rising sun does not discriminate, and what it likes best to do, is come again, the next day.

Mallarme, a single thing I want from you. And that is your being to be free, as free as you like, or as little. It is up to you. You have earnt it. Your great words, and your life. Do not be displeased.

Having a walk in the garden. It is little known, that this garden is where the ashes of a king are spread. It is little known that his queen's hand still plays a part in our lives. We must away.

Mallarme, do you dare belong with the rest of us? Do you see forever, with your almond eyes? Have you the pleasure of the name in times of difficulty. This is your lot, and our plan.

Digging in, before the flames have broken. Witnessing the dawn for one more time. How many times have you seen the dawn? Is it something you do? I hope it is, I hope it is more than me.

Mallarme – draw closer, draw near, as near as you can reckon, and then back, back again, until we reach the equilibrium of the age. There is here more than we had hoped.

A gathering of rose petals! A gathering of floods. And here where we are lost without a trace, there is new hope, hope that springs from some ungodly place. And now, we must run!

Mallarme, have you come for us, for our need? When there is nothing left, there is nothing left – this much is clear. There can only be the weathering of a thousand ships.

Swinging into unknown places. We perceive ourselves to be in line with so much. There is never enough to truly be. There is never enough to hold on. When we are free, we will be.

Mallarme – are you strong? Are you strong enough to sail into places unseen, places unexpected? And now, when we have a raft to put together, we will be that thing that never dies.

There is, in this land, a forthright conviction, that believes in all it wants, and has the gumption to handle foreign climes, with the strength of five hundred men. Do not be here.

Mallarme – you are the one we want. Your steel is our steel, your shoes, ours. There comes a burgeoning forth, that unwinds as it masquerades. Come, do not be afraid, there is more.

A vista that we have never seen. A hallway, that leads to the wreck. A humming that does not know time. We are free here, free to choose our destiny. Be the one that never fails.

MALLARME

Mallarme, a ringing true – a sense to hear ourselves through the throng. There is what is in us from the start, but where is that? We will never surrender ourselves to the night.

There is a forest here, that let's in no light. There are sounds, that shed no delight. Be the morning, and the sun will have your wish. Be the sounds and sights of spring, and yours will be all.

Mallarme – are you the one to linger? Are you the one to stay true, true to the light that guides the way? Are you, my Mallarme, the one not to falter, always to rise, again and again?

Has the lingering sky-line not taken to the shore? How many wisps of smoke do you see? I see none, which is good. I see the treasured road as a gift, and not a blessing.

Mallarme, there is a song. It ruffles us, but that is okay. It sees what we don't, and has earth as an accompaniment. There is a flash, and we are there. Do you see it, my Mallarme?

Finding the gift in amongst the blackberry bush. Finding the way home. Finding that which is alone, and bringing it near. There is sand here, but we will move forward still.

Mallarme – a winter that knows of no harbour. A summer that knows of no arbour. There is light here, like never before. Have the merriment as your own, you will entice.

Forgiving, and being in the moment. Transpiring, and then arriving. Being transfixed, and being encumbered. There are times when we must away, and times when we must stay.

Mallarme – do you come from beneath? Do you stare at the heavens, and know them to be essential? What is this you say? Do you hear, or are you soft? The measure is in the wind.

Come and be placated. Be the wishing on the stone. Be the trample in the maze. Come for the benevolence, and be that which can only linger. Longings that trace, and are gone.

Mallarme – have you seen the rub, the rub of the stars? Have you heard more than your fair share? Has the dawn not lingered enough? Has the sun been too shallow to mark time?

Catching hold, and never letting go. Being cleverer than the rest. Knowing how to continue, and never giving in. Knowing what is best, and believing it to be true. Being sustained.

Mallarme – are you a tether, that does not fly down? Can you hurry like the wind in winter? Is it enough that we have time together? Is it enough, that the way we see is clear?

Married in the key, sizing up the future. Being in touch with so much. Believing once again in things. Having heart, being alive. Alive to the now, alive to the sustenance of the soul.

Mallarme – a dream! A faraway place! Nearness, like a spring of water! And then, something we don't expect. Something that leaves us lounging. Not to be longed for, nor feathered.

Catching the wave before it departs. Having more of the sound of it, the sound of it under. Belligerent and with guile, there is no place left. There is no time to depart now.

MALLARME

Mallarme – watching, waiting – being in touch. Having a hold on the voice, and then being of the centre. Do not depart from this place alone, there are things here that do not weep.

A strange sound, that emits no note. A feather that does not float. Which way to turn, it is uncertain? Which way to call home, and then we can rest. Valuing everything and everybody.

Mallarme, a thing to be found, a thing to be sought. What is heavier than the round? What is more pleasant than the type-set? What do we do here, despite ourselves? Come, and be forgiven.

What is more than this? What is less than the sand on a deserted beach? Come to the land, and see it through. Come to the point of deliverance, and know the key for what it is.

Forgetting the mantle of things. Being in the hub, and for the rub. Do not be afraid there are things that guide. There is now something for us, that knows how to sleep and how to make friends.

Mallarme – do be strong, be as strong as you can be. There is more here than we can reckon. The distance is alive, alive with the fecund. Be the march, and yours will be the night.

Holding the flag aloft, and knowing its importance. Being in sight of the loft, as it comes again in unison. Having the courage to keep going, despite it all. Having what is left.

A nestling place, that knows only itself. Who is there to blame, where blame is useless. Who is there to be, when being is at an end. Who is there to see, when seeing shines.

Mallarme – a sense I have that things will right themselves. New born life that has a say. What is there to do, when doing is strained? Have the rest of us, we will come. Be in, and be true.

Going deep, into the world – what is at its heart? It is difficulty. What is of its soul? Difficulty. Before we are through, we will experience all sorts of things. Well, all sorts of difficulty. But we will succeed!

Mallarme – are you the wanderer through lands untold? Are you the sentence in the middle of the paragraph? Do not bend here, it will not be to your liking. Like steel, and the rod.

Munificence, and the heart. Be still my wandering one, be like the wind – there, and then not. Be like a heart, that beats in time to the drums of a thousand nights labour, and then?

Mallarme – do you climb, unto ridges untold? Do you listen to the beat of the night in ranging form? Is there more in you than the drum can maintain? Do not be here, it will not suit.

What is left of the food for the gulls? What do we see, when seeing is enough? What do we find, when the finding we have equates to the hearth? Be the one who lingers, it will help.

Mallarme, is your soul a banquet, that cannot be satiated? Do you stand on ridges high enough to break any fall? Is there land between your feet, and the summit of any mountain?

MALLARME

Without the slightest concern, there is a leaf that blows across the grandeur. There is here, without care, a newly found respite. It lingers, and does what is true. But what of us?

Mallarme – do you speak, speak in unholy ways; I can't believe it – no! This is the weather of us, as we seek once again to shield our eyes from things untold – and then, away.

Reaching to see more – reaching to be in the right place. And then, without recompense, we fathom the bottom of the sea, and know it to be deep. Just this once.

Mallarme, a thing to see. A thing that does not shift. A thing that harbours nothing – no feeling of remorse, no little tune asunder. Be the one Mallarme, be the one and find more.

This is the balustrade where I sit, and know no fear. This is the time it takes to wander further than anyone has before. I see the light train upon me, but I have no desire.

Mallarme – are you the night? Are you the daylight that holds the night at bay? Does your seam catch on the ream of things? Do you liken yourself to the horizon, a thing that does not sleep?

There are things here that have no say, no say in the way we go. But there's is the fight, as ours is the witness to simple daydreaming, and all that will come to pass. Be the in-between of things, yes.

Mallarme, are you the chorus that has no fruit? Are you the wellbeing that lies atop the rafters. Be the sense of things, there is time. Be what is, and yours will be the gluttony of the air.

Forests in density. Foreboding that thrives. And when the daylight comes, there will be a time to dance to no music, and to no sound. This is what we live for, and what we exonerate most often.

Mallarme – do you see as far as we, as far as we can see? Is your ball on the chain, or around its base? Do you love the way we confide in each other? Is this the way it lurches?

A wanting that has no soul, and no tune to give. A courtship of clouds, that has as its anchor the treasure of existence. And then with hands replete, nothing more to say, and nothing more to do.

Mallarme – are you fair? Do you see the day for what it is? Is yours what we cannot see, nor can feel? The lust of the stars is here to forgive, so let it do its work. Let us not pertain to anything, that is fair.

Let the moon cast its ameliorating rays down corridors as sleek as dust, and as troublesome as oils and canvas. There are things we must do here, to seek, and to find.

Mallarme – there is less of the marching, and more of the soul. There is less of the changing light, and more of the density of things. We seek forever, but what does that mean?

MALLARME

Holding back the tears, giving life to nothingness. Have we, in the fullness of time, been too late to thrive? I don't think so, but that is not what we have in store! Come we will swim.

Mallarme – is this the point of no return; I believe it is – then let us not so much as enjoy ourselves, as furnish to the light here with an almighty aplomb. One that does not seek itself.

There is pleasure somewhere here – I have heard its footsteps in dead of night. But fleeting as it is, I am sure we will cross paths again, if only in the distant future. Be assured.

Mallarme – to see again, to witness the dawn, as she sleeps, and then awakes! There is nothing more to live for that this ritual, of the namesake and the distant that comes close.

A further doing that lets the light in. What is more, but not less. What is in the mile, and the stone – what we gather for ourselves, and ourselves only. We will be what we want to be.

Mallarme – are you here? Are you here amongst the rouble? The sticks that bind a way. Are we the ones to be let through, let through the base to the summit? There can be more than this.

Further insight, further truth – do our minds work the same? I should think in lesser compartments, there is lesser thought. We are there, you and I, we are the one's not to shirk.

Mallarme – do you laugh as well? Is your joking a solid rasp on steel? Is this where we lie, on the backs of soldiers past? There can only be one way – and that is through.

Furthering the light on its course through the night. Having a handle on so much, that we can't see clearly. Of all that we have, of all that we have lost – there is nothing left to do.

Mallarme – are you strong? Are we weak? Is there a piece of the future nestled away here? Can we once again ride our horse, unto the field, unto the road? There is a trail here, we will use it.

Looking for the right way to enter. Feeling like we had had a past, and then revoked it. What is more, we are here tonight, and will not go anywhere else. The past is here, but what of the present?

Mallarme – do we place our hands down to win? Do we feather our pillows with ash, and know it to be the most comfortable thing here? What is more delightful than the light of day? We shall see.

A nestling close. A memory that has many victories. We harvest memories like a tomb, and know that the last is yet to come. Don't be one, be many, it will suit the times.

Mallarme – are you in need of something to calm you? That is good, because there is nothing here. Do you sleep on a bed of tight ropes, that gain nothing from your ease?

Forests of forgetfulness, treasures that don't know their name. A feast that is in no one's honour. A opening that slides us forward, and knows how to begin. What is this, I hear you ask?

MALLARME

Mallarme – there is never a chance like this. Never a chance like this to be what we want to be, and do it all. There is a kiss here, a kiss that leaves no breath behind, nor stasis to wink!

What is here?! What is on the brim of it? There is life in this chest, heart in this beating, feathers in this row. There cannot be anything more, anything more, than love in the chamber.

Mallarme – is this your future? Is this what you have in store for the birds, birds of prey that do not bite? In this we are thankful, that no single person can be the twilight more than you.

Having the snow, and being a part of the show. Rapscallion, and the never mind belief. There is here a new sort of thing, one that never gives in, and always fights to the last.

Mallarme, do you see what others can't? Do you descend upon high to rally the mass? Is this the way we come, from north to south, and then forwards again? Let us fly!

Having quite the time of it, and being centred all the while. There is never more than we can show, never in the land of the dreaming man. There is fun here, and excitement!

Mallarme, do the clouds flock under your wing? Is there moisture, so that we may see the way? Can the driven and the perplexed align in unity, so that there is nothing left to do?

Hoping like never before, that what the future bestows is what we had hoped for. There is nothing like the wind to have a say, and the sunlight to bring us home. Yes, indeed.

Mallarme – are you the one to weep tears of fortitude? Is there nothing in the wind to tell us of this? Hoping and straining, being at one with the night. Can we never relinquish the time?

Oftentimes we see ourselves like the magic it takes to battle a fish until it has won. There can be no other way, than this. There can be nothing other than this, in the chamber of life.

Mallarme – the whetstone is allowed to speak – but what does it speak of? It speaks of the history of things, of the future of things; the in-between of things, and the outside of things.

Accidental traveller, singing like the road has no turns. Be the weather, in a strange land, and yours will be the undertaking of a lifetime. Have no more to say, and the strange land will fill you.

Mallarme – a new seed. One to water, and let grow. One to see in the meadow, as its height increases. Do not weather the storm in levity, there is much to be done, and much to be undone.

Foraging around in the attic, I see what is to come. It is so difficult, and so out of touch with what I am used to. But we will persist, and see what comes about, and then, a shout!

Mallarme – are you in touch? Are you the speed, and not the danger? Does your vision build on its strength? Does the night time wandering of a thousand inches speak to the dawn?

MALLARME

Flippancy, and all that time can curtail. The destiny of each star in the sky, including ours. A density for living truths, that has as its alter, all that is, and all that is not. Do not belie the sand, it will sting.

Mallarme – have we gone further than ever before? Have we turned on touchstone's heart, a movement that sends us sprawling into the forever, and then back again? We won't part again.

Overarching, and never missing. Balustrades that only let us tumble. What we have fought for, and will never relinquish. Only what is left, will placate. Only what is left. Yes.

Mallarme – is the sound yours? The sound of talking on the balcony? To this we say, 'amiss'. To this we say, 'through, and around, and up and down'. There is nothing like it.

Come and play, with the great Mallarme! Come and witness history for the undertaking. Be a pleasure, without a pain (rare). Be a wellspring before the tempest.

Mallarme – do you sing now? – Of course not. Not now, that things are spread and already eaten. Do not cast the time it takes to carry on in such a fashion – we will win, you and I.

Going out into the wilderness, never to return. With this acceptance, we depart, and never look back. And now a simple cry – never give in. That's right – never give in. There it is written.

A flagstaff in the middle of it. One we cannot see properly, for all the people there – some are sitting, some are lying supine, some are standing. And a lone flagstaff in the middle.

Mallarme – is this the way? Is this the way through? Can we see ourselves properly when we are through? Is there more than ever to see once we are there? We shall see.

Mallarme – oneiric and with passion, something to strive for, and something to be in tune for. There is always a new place to go, a new place to see – always. And then, well yes.

Gathering to keep abreast of the times. Feeling the ancient wonder of it all. Sensing, that in the future there will be more to come. Silence, that has as its base, the suffering of the world.

Mallarme – do you sing with cradle detached? Are you the sounding board for a generation? Is this the way it will be, caught in amongst it, until tears run down our cheeks?

There is a misguiding insight that keeps watch over the night. It tells us to be free, and then wrenches that freedom from us with all of its might. There can never be a sign so great.

Mallarme – where were you in the middle of it all? Where were you hiding? No you weren't hiding, you were out an about, and wishing for the daylight to be yours for the fight.

There is more between you and your mate than you think. But what of it, everything here is good, everything here is line with things, and everything here does what is expected.

Mallarme – do you sense what I sense? Do you feel what I feel? Is this where things don't end, but simply begin? We

MALLARME

will come for the daylight, and stay for the laughter. This is us.

A never ending ride, one that leaves nothing to the imagination. One so ingrained with truth, that the night we have, is more like a dream than we had a first thought. Come, yes.

Mallarme – do you see our souls entranced? Is there nothing which to live by? Is the turn of events stranger than the mile? Do we clasp on, so that our sides do not split, and carry us?

All the more for the light. It nourishes us before tutelage time has come. And now, when the voice of the sky opens to say what is what, here a solemn breeze, that has nothing left.

Mallarme – I sense your displeasure. But that is okay, there can be nothing more to drag you into the fight. But there is no fight here. Nothing to send us backwards as well as forwards.

A solid whim, that has as its shine new time, and ancient wonder. There is in us now a sort of placating motion, that believes in silk, and all she will carry. Be the motion, and you will have all.

Mallarme, do you send your harp away, like all good musicians, or do you twirp still further? I know what I am doing, now that I have a say! There is a just timbre that does not resonate.

Having trouble seeing the page, but this does not matter. Further and further from the shore, I go, and am placated. I see no one here, but that is just part of my making.

Mallarme – listen to the chores we have, they speak of love and loss, and all kinds of in-between. There is here, now, a kind of reticence to be feathered – and all that it will bring.

What we never thought possible, after the time it took for the rags to dry on the afternoon stone. There is never more than we can hold. There is only this, and this only.

Mallarme – do you find yourself amiss, awash with words, even now? Do you hear what the doe brings? It is a gift for you in your dotage. But what have we to bring? Much more, besides.

Catching a glimpse of the moon, and its heavenly arc. What we never believed, until now. There are times that are sweet, and times that are bitter, and it is up to us to decide which we have.

Mallarme – do you sweat? Is your garb clean? Do you run that extra mile? Are all things equal? Does the right word approach, as if by magic? Do you believe in sounds outdated?

There is grace in these years, grace that belies the foreboding. Do not be uncertain of the path we tread. It is not the oration to deaf ears that startles us, it is something more, and something less.

Mallarme – do you fret? Do you cast a slow bow towards the sky? There is enough to keep us going, and that is enough. Do not show speed here, it will only bark that little bit more.

There are things that should show themselves to be a right, and there are things that should be left alone, left to their

MALLARME

own chosen seat. There is a feather in the way, we will move it.

Mallarme – are you alone? Do you need companionship, in the water of things? Do you need that urbane cup, from which to sup? Gather up our miserly things, and go forth.

Happiness – Eudaimonia. Is it a myth? Or what is it? Is it something which will torture us for not having it. Better to be without suffering, than hanker after the grand positive – happiness.

Mallarme – do you lounge with great abandon, now that you are there? Do you see yourself amongst the timbers of a lost forest, with an art museum in a clearing in the middle.

Thought, beside ourselves. What is here, is not there. What comes in the night, only comes once. Do we dare dream, dream of the still lake, where it all began? This much we can do.

Mallarme – does the sand stop at your toes, never to reach your legs? Do things stay the same for you, forever onwards. Are you the draft of shadows, that heads into more?

A crisis unfolds, and we are here. A dilapidated old cottage holds the key. And here, where we linger nightly, there is a chance once again to bring up the rear, and have a whisper.

Mallarme – do you sound like the ages in the story book? Is yours a sycamore dance? Is yours a true word, that never gives in. Is this what we fight for? Is this what we win?

Forcing the door to our dreams, we move carefully forwards. They are all here, and I can see them. It matters not, they will act, and act in due course. We must let them breathe.

Mallarme – holding on to things, ever so slightly. There is the time it takes, that can only be measured by an old fob watch that stands in the middle of so much, so much. We will come.

Coming in from all sides, we tread our way to the very top, and then shout a new name from the rooftops of existence. There is always something new, and always something of the adventure.

Mallarme – is this what we have come for? Is this what we have paid our price for? I have never in all my times had a time like this. But that is okay, we are here to do a job – let us do it!

And then, when the sea is of the correct level, new besmirching smiles that harbour no dreams. But what is the dream, and why has it come? There will be nothing more to see.

Mallarme – have you seen what I have seen? Have you been to places I have been? This is what I say now – be gone, and never return, oh dark clouds. There will be something more.

What is it we seek? What is it we find, when we have climbed the last bastion? There is something that we don't understand, something deep. We cannot get to it, for all our fumbling.

MALLARME

Mallarme, are you replete with strength? Do you dive that once more, to see things clearly? Is this the way we go, up and then down, and then around again. Mallarme, do you see?

Come and be amazed at it all. Come and be that thing which troops as it saunters. Be the missive in the rain. Be something we don't understand, and your gift will be here.

Mallarme – come and see us at play. There is moisture here, so we can be ourselves freely. Never come to this place with people, there isn't room for anyone else. Be true.

There is more space here, than we had ever thought. We can saddle our horses, right here. We can find space for growing things, but what of the rest? What of the same in all of us. We will see.

Mallarme – Do you have the life, to match your words? That is important. I think you do, but let us look through history. What torments have writers suffered – your hero, Baudelaire!

Longing for the night, I see the road ahead. In the distance, a town, one that hasn't seen a visitor in a thousand years. I move towards it, readying myself for what comes next…

Mallarme – Yours is the readiness, the readiness for all. Be the division of souls, and yours will be the vapour and the mask. Be all that you can be, and your cleansing will be one of the ages.

Come for the play, stay for the ball. We will have the greatest of times. There will not be a thing left. Not one thing to settle our stance by. Be entrusted with the boon, it will not hurt.

Mallarme – Seething, and with persistence, there lies a great treasure. The moon is full, but what of the plains? Do we sense that thing again, that has no remorse? What is it?

What reason do we have, to plumb the depths, and season the horse we ride? There cannot be a whetstone here, only something that barks in trepidation through the mist.

Mallarme – do you swing about on tresses made for looking at? Do you start again like fire on ice? There can never be anything more than fondness and the clerk. Be the stable door, but do not open yourself.

Catching the last rays of sun in the evening dusk. Preparing to get up for the dawn. There is never anything more than this. Never anything more we can do. We will not hurry.

Mallarme – is your walk brisk? Do you delight in the way of things? Is your spontaneity like fibres from the sun? Do you ravish the day, so that your sound knows no boundaries?

Raising our ink stained hands in welcome. There are places we will go to that do not know their names. But what is it we seek there? There is never enough time in the day.

Mallarme – are your signs enough? Are you the one to tread on eggshells, and have them not break? Do you see the further horizon, but are unsure how to move it? Come now, we must away.

MALLARME

Gathering for the family photo – your black and white is perfect Mallarme, but what of the dawn? What colours can we capture there? We must not hide from the colours of life!

Mallarme – do you charge into the fray? Have you the rainbow, and not the bile? Is yours the source, and the never ending? I hope not, but that is okay. Belittle nothing here.

Hearing the sound of the ranch, we linger only in so far as things right themselves. And then, when we know what it is worth, we will come in staggers of gold, blisses of white.

Mallarme – There are places unseen, people unmet. But do not hold court with the lovers, theirs is a difficult journey. Be withheld no more, we will come for you in dead of night.

Fashioning a garb, out of what is left. Stretching the boundaries of things. Never giving in. Never giving in. Always fighting for the end. And in the finish, and new type of life.

Mallarme – are you the one to see with straight eyes. Do you love what you see? Is there more to life than this? Can we see with the betterment of spirit, and all that will come to pass?

There are rails here, rails to hold on to. They are things we see when we first awake in the morning, that may be all blurry, but they are there to guide us. Do not be afraid, you will see them soon.

Mallarme, is yours the troupe, and the swagger? Is yours the nails made of paint? Is this your chance at remembering – remembering all that came about? Do you remember Mallarme?

Catching with fondness, we look out into the yard, and talk of times gone past. What is here, never used to be here. What is now lost, has always been so. What we cannot find, will never remain so.

Mallarme – are you the tinker of souls? Are you the sentience in the sea, or its seeming passage through worlds untold? Do not brace yourself Mallarme, there are things to harvest.

Having fare, but not enjoying it. Being capable, and then throwing yourself in. What is there left, left to feed the gulls? What is there left, that does not catch itself in the making?

Mallarme – do you curse the embers of every worn down fire? Is yours the ineptitude of desire? Be of a rancour, there is no other way. Be of the sand of the dunes, and yours will be illimitable.

There is a crossing, that marks the spot. The spot where we lay for the very first time. And at this crossing, there is a bird, a minor bird, that knows no other way. See, it comes.

Mallarme – Is it like hands, hands that span? Is it the gust of wind that never seems to still? Can you raise your arm up, until it reaches the sky? There will be more to come, this much is assured.

And then, a flame that cannot go out. Nothing in the world can put it out. And then, before our unbelieving eyes, a dance. A dance that loves as it embraces. There can be nothing more than this.

MALLARME

Mallarme – do you wish sometimes for the breadth of it? For something to startle you into believing. There is more than we can know, but with quiet resolve, we can understand what we have.

There is time to know, and time to be free. What is this that I ask of you, Mallarme? It is of the inkling, and the shard. It is you and I, as we walk again amongst embers of worn down worlds.

Mallarme – do you see yourself? Not your visage in the mirror, but to the depths of your soul? This is where we must look, if we are to be placated. And here, where we are again, we rest, and find solace.

And just hanging there, a bowl of fruit! What has it come for? Where is it going? It just hangs there – we must ask the owner if we can have some! Yes, and here all. Yes.

Mallarme – do you sense the change? Do you know what is coming? It is a train to all that. Yes this is the way forward – to catch that train, and take that journey, and be that thing – here, there is whiteness in your eyes, whiteness that bleeds no truth. Come let us go.

Holding on, for forever, never letting go, always dissolving never absolving. Giving the round-a-bout what it needs to keep us spinning. Yes that is it, spinning, and whirling, and, well yes, never letting go.

Mallarme – do you swim the mile? Do you race the serpent through the enclave? And is this your last race? Can you catch up that one last time? We wish you well, and hope you come with us.

Feeling like there was no more. Being in touch with so much. Having to hang on, despite the feeling. In there, and through. Coming full circle. Believing, but not intrigued.

Mallarme – do you sense your fate? Is it in reams of gold? Does it fence of the world, and then let it come through? There is no dream like it. There is no time to prepare, so we go.

What is never quite like the rest. What comes to calm. What does not sleep. What has no motion. What sees no sound, and hears no ocean. We will have it here, the two of us.

Mallarme – do we sing at full breath? Do we not deny our origin? Are we ensnared by the beauty of it? Does this compare to that? Are we in full swagger? Can we dance again?

Just around the corner, and down the road, there is a place that harbours all that we fear, and all that we know. It is to this place we come, time and time again. But now, no fear.

Mallarme, do you wait for night? Are you in line with the tiger? Does your standing belie your fate? Do not come here during the daylight, it is far too easy. Only come for forgiveness.

Having the sand, and wishing for the dune. There is now, in this place, a kind of calm, that knows only itself, and is not a keeper. Be in touch with more of this place, and you will not compromise.

Mallarme – are you the one to be like the rest? I should think not, my brave knight. There are places amongst the rubble where we might not be so perturbed. Come now, let us see.

MALLARME

Where is the motion that we seek? What drives us ever onwards? Do we bark at the sight of it? Do we have what is near, so that we may be far? Never understanding, we march, until closeness.

Mallarme, can you see yourself in pleasant garb, such that you can see more? There is a time in every journey when the light dims, and the way is only marked by thin torches.

The gesticulations of a wise man. This man does not know the way, he cannot direct us, he knows only what the back of his hand can tell him, and yet it is his job to tell us what is next.

Mallarme – we hold on, as tight as we can, and knowing that light is a beacon for us, we continue on, staff in hand, with heat resplendent. There can be only this, and this only.

Graduating plains, that come from nowhere. Being in the middle of it despite ourselves. An openness that transcends. What we never thought to fight for, and now must.

Mallarme, is this the time to despair? Is this the time we must sally forth, riding at breakneck speed? Do we find ourselves wandering even further through the marshes?

Having hope, it is all we can do. Having that which will hold us in good stead. Being able to run, and then walk, and then be content if we can, if not, then run wild and free.

Mallarme, are you placed as you wish? Do you now come close to the beginning? What is it about this place that has walls instead of rooves, and tiles instead of boards?

There is a line in the sand we must not cross. And here, where the hour glass does not chime, there will be a recompense that bears no salt. Be in line with the rest, and there will be no course.

Mallarme, do you stand, or do you fall? You stand! Do you come, or are you waylaid? Who would be ready for that? And now, a new force, that comes into play, now that everything is quiet.

Is everything fine? Does the sun become your charge? Is there a nicety we have missed? Come now, sing along with us, there is a new bride. Someone who the mist has not shaken.

Mallarme – is yours in the milk of life? Do you falter before acceptances? Is now the time to head for the trees? Do not be afraid, we have only come for the bird's nest, as it ceases.

This is what we have come for. To see the wreck and let it encompass us. And here, where we are so brisk, a new feather to bind us to the meal. Do not be afraid, we cannot.

Mallarme – is your season one of laughter, or one of tears? Let us say, laughter, and then tell a joke, a joke to settle us. Is this the way you have come, in jovial delight? Come, yes.

There is in this space, a place, that bears no design nor intrepid disaster. There is here, rather, a mingling, of the old and new, of the up and down, and the sideways and the straight.

MALLARME

Mallarme – do you last the feathered dance? Do you wish for the things which do not come? Is yours a parlance that relinquishes the time for the day? Come now and do not fear, it will care.

Something has a hold on us, something special. We will not limit our embrace to all that is, any longer. We will come for the laughter, and not for the special insistence, not now.

Mallarme – is yours the time to come in waves, as ours is the way that often bites? Do we see the way forward, and through, and inside? Is this the way we fly to new places, and beyond?

There is time, more time than we had thought possible. There is time to harvest, to be, to enjoy, to salvage what is left – to do, to seek, to wander, to have at our beck and call.

Mallarme – are you what is left of us, left of the round and the sound? There can only be one night left, one night and the clover. Wearing clothes that do not fit, we ride again.

This is how we find ourselves, when the finding is a forge at work. This is how the song completes the verse, and over and amongst. Do not shirk here, there is an end to this completion.

Mallarme, there is a sort of thing that brings nothing with it. Who would have thought this to be possible? Who would have foreseen this? There is now nothing left – but wait, more!

What do we see, when we look? What is it that draws us onward? It is the sea, that harbours no flame – it is the night, that sees only itself. We must run there, just to see what is.

Mallarme – do you know what you seek? Is there time enough to see the future? Do we always come to grief at this point? We must not see ourselves any differently? Do you?

This is where I met the tutelage of daffodils. This is where spring had come, a spring of the soul. There is never much we can see here – only that which has Neptune in the semblance of things.

Mallarme – are you offset? Do you talk in tangential wanderings? Is the game required here one of strength? Can we never know what we must seek? This much, and more.

Closer to the end than the beginning, we saddle up nearing the starlit shore. And then, without the forest moon, there comes a stillness, a stillness that does not break. And here we find ourselves.

Mallarme, Mallarme, are you a ranger in a far out land? Do you stick to the promise you made to your mother – to stay safe? Do you run that extra distance, so that none may catch you?

Happening in the spaces. Being last, and then first. Being like it never was. Having the courage. Being in the middle, and then on the outside. Having what is left. Deciding.

Mallarme – there is news, my great one. There is news from the abode. What does it tell of? It tells of success, and new times, it tells of much besides. It tells of what we could always be.

MALLARME

And here, in the straight, there is a ship that cannot sink. It keeps buoyant throughout the journey, by one single thought – adventure! That will see it through. Yes.

Mallarme – are you the one to go on living? Are you the one to know what's best? Do you see yourself in the mirror, and smile? Do you know the places you have been, and are pleased?

There is a new chance to fathom the sea. But what will we find? We will find more than we could have hoped. You see, it is at the bottom of the sea where dreams are fashioned.

Mallarme – do not grieve, yours is the toil and the broth. Yours is the testing and the strength. Yours is the vast panorama and the ocean. Yours is what is next, and what is now.

There is a noise, that does not make a sound. There is a place, that knows only itself. There are tensions that lead to revival. There is nothing left here, except the new.

Mallarme – are you the one who knows how to be? Are you the one who knows how to know? Can we be that thing which we have always wanted to be? Can we be that thing?

There is never the sort of paling to keep the fence shut. There will always be what we hoped, we simply must wait, and look that little closer. The fence is to keep us out, but what about in?

Mallarme – do you smile on the inside, so that we do not know how to look at you? Do you wish us to talk to you in tongues? Do you have the chosen field before you, so that you can run through it?

What is in the water, is not in the way. What comes into the field from the bastion, is not of our concern. We look for other ways to proceed, but this is the only way. We will be on our own.

Mallarme – do you see yourself in dreams of black? Do you disappoint, only to succeed? Is this the way you come at things, now that the straight is cut off? Bend a little.

There is one more chance, and then we are through. Do we take our time, or quickly move into position? Do we have time to blow a last kiss, or do we not know which way to turn?

Mallarme – this is the wind, and here is the sand. The sea stands guard, as the ruined and ancient castle looks on. There are no trees here, no place to rest your horse.

There is never time for tears here! There is only time for what is best, and not what is worst. Come now, we must be all we can, and we must sally forth unto the land of dreams.

A sideways glimpse of beauty and all she entails. This is what I am hoping for in this book. Has it been achieved? Only you can tell; the reader. I am but the emissary. Yes.

Mallarme – winding down on fate, there is a noise that does not languish. And here, where the land is in partial eclipse, there can be more to us than ever before. Yes, please come.

Mallarme – do you winnow with regret, that what was told to you, was only half the story. There are now many seams, many threads, to let us reach full of the capacity of our elders. Yes, come.

The effort we put in, is not enough to see things through. But wait, a solution! There are things we don't understand, and things we see in the mirror, things that only remind us of life.

Mallarme – you are resplendent in your garb. Your light is like the narrowness of fortune. Be the whole, and the part will win you over. Be the transient insistence, and yours will be something to believe in.

There is something here we don't understand. It is like the race had been completed before time. There is now a simplicity, and a movement. A sorrowful tune, and all that was.

Mallarme – there is the way of it, and there is the soulful embrace. Is this what we have come for, my dear Mallarme? Is this what has brought us here, to this place of completion?

Holding aloft the embrace of time! Being in the middle of something special. Coaching the hills to give up their greenness. And then, doing as we wish until the time has elapsed.

Mallarme – do you see what we all see, and that is hope? Do you come in from the cold, to be simply as we. We will not languish anymore in these rooms, these rooms of complaint.

There are things that do not cry. There are places that launch in the untold, never to remit. There now, do not ponder. We have fought a mighty battle in our sleep, and now come once again.

Mallarme – are you the chance in the night, the sail to sail by? Is this the way to go, before all places, before all peoples? Can we see once again, just like nothing had happened?

The temperance and the sleigh. It is winter, and the snow has fallen on the heights. Do not let the belligerence of the hills rain down on you. There can only be one thing to do, and that is lift ourselves.

Mallarme – is this the storm that is no tempest? Is this the shinning of things untold? Where is the light, when things are here in gold? We listen, but for what? What is it we see with our own eyes?

The depths of it, are shallow. The nearness of it – far. The likeness of it – stunned. The hopefulness of it – entailed. What will we be, but all, but everything we can be, and more.

Mallarme, do you rise to your challenge? Do you seek assistance from the light? Is it forthcoming? Is it in the midst of a great adventure? This thing called life. Now, we must away.

Listening like the sky, and hearing what is never enough. Being in force, and not in decay. What there is in the distance between this and that. Walking in time to the beat of life's drum.

Mallarme – is this the rule, and the sober reflection? Is the way forward, or the way backward? Do you calm yourself in springs of not being sure? Is this the way we have to see it?

MALLARME

And then, the trouble passes, and a new light comes, comes in full swagger, in unperturbed nuance. Be not troubled, it says, yours of the softness and the guile. Yes.

Mallarme – is this the starting point, of something made of gold, of silver, and of twine? Can we push ourselves forward in the crevice of the daylight wandering? Yes we can.

The dress and the plain, the forwards, and the backwards. What is made of steel, cannot be bent – What is made of sea shells, cannot be heard – What is made of rose, cannot be smelt.

Mallarme – are you plunging into things? Do you have a hold on life, that does not diminish? Is this the way you travel, through the inside and the out? Do not be alarmed.

There are trees not to climb, and places not to be. But here, where the danger is palpable, there is a certain quiet, that knows how to react. In sweetness, and in temperance.

Mallarme – is yours the major to the minor? Does yours smell of the ground, in all its forms? Can we tell something is quiet, when the noise subsides from the day? Be with us.

Holding on to hope, there is more in the trees than we had first thought. There can be only composure, and aplomb, in the middle of all our wandering. Never let go, always persist.

Mallarme – the dreams we have cannot be snuffed out, they only get larger, and in more fully developed strain. The things we are sure of, remain so. But what of life? Well, yes.

Hiding in the middle of the square, life and all its accoutrements, can never be found. There is only one thing to be known, and that is not for the faint hearted. Come, we will see what comes.

Mallarme – sing to us. Be of that sort that knows no sound. Be of the enclave of life, as if patters on stones untold. Be of the wellspring, and the tiding, and all that will be. Be up for it.

The heart of it, the sound of it – the moisture that wells up in our eyes. Everything it takes, and more. We will not give in, and not stop, and not placate for any person. Yes.

Mallarme – to dive within, and find the solution, this much is said in the dark. There are places untold to the living, but they are not captured by the light. We will, with furrowed brow, begin.

Hoping in the meantime, that our story would remain so. But this is neither here, nor there – what is important is the trajectory of the outright, that does not sail for any port mapped, or not.

Mallarme – sing us a lullaby, so that we might sleep to a new tune. Do not puff your eyes into shapes of weeping arbour. Only, and for some, these are wanted, but we must only be here.

The sizeable, and the dimensional, ride in swift glide through the parts amassing, and into what awaits. The silence is a thing worth crying for, and the road is a thing worth crossing for.

MALLARME

Mallarme – are you entwined with twine, so that you cannot escape? Does the life you lead now, encompass you, so you have to fall on pretty flowers? Come now, we must not wait.

There, in the space between things, there, there is where it is. What we have looked for all this time. It never moves, it always moves. This thing without a name. We have found it!

Mallarme – do you sense the reason behind the talk? Do you know how often this has played out? Do you veer from left to right, or do you stay on track? Is there enough to see us through?

There is a play thing called life. It emits no odour, and carries no transit. There it sits, wholesome and reposed. Do we believe in no other thing than this? There are more questions than answers.

Mallarme – do you sit in comfortable seating? Are you the one to take the night there? Is this what we seek, the night? Lit with a full moon, and always taken in, the night, the night.

Galvanised by the world. Sitting on the edge of things. Being capable and not afraid. Being in the midst of all that is. Being capricious, but only to remain on track. There is more, there is more.

Mallarme – is this the land we seek? Is this the shoreline that holds the ancient wreck? Is there a listening beyond all things? Do we swim for long distances, never to tire?

A new land, one to absolve the old. There is enough of tricks here, enough to see us through. In this place, a chasm, a chasm that only laughs. It laughs at us, as we go about our daily business.

Mallarme – the whetstone sharpens our life. The whetstone that feels no heat, and only sharpens what is needed. Are we needed, my friend? I hope so, yes we are, this much I know.

The feather and the ride. The horses do not gallop, but casually trot. We are at liberty to talk of things unknown, things unsaid. And here, where we find ourselves, some respite.

Mallarme – the whistle and the blast. What we have come for, but the trickling down of tired limbs, and windswept hearts. There can only be a never before seen adventure.

In the middle of it all, a new sense that things will be okay. In the middle of it all, an old belief, that the right way is up. In the middle of it all, a sparrow as it chimes with fervour.

Mallarme – the heart of it does not flinch. The heart of it, my friend, my much longed for friend, the heart of it is here. It is in between us, and cannot be traded for anything.

Pleasing the people around us, just so we can say we have been there. Being in wonder, such that it hurts. Being in the wilderness, and not treating them any differently.

Mallarme – do you know what it takes? Do you surmise all that you are after, and never look back? Do you wonder about the sky, and know that it can never have you?

The fight is for the night – let's leave them to it. There is never a right time in any of this. There is only a pool of rain water left for the birds to play in. Let us leave this place, never to return.

Mallarme – is this what we see seek? Is this the time of day we record for our own devices? Never in the shallows of deliverance have we been so calm. Yes, we will come, but never again.

The trees, and the forest, and the light between the stones. There is a waterfall here, one that never stops, for any person, with any authority. It is like it has the power of sand, never diminishing, only moving.

Mallarme – on the mat, there lays a bull. On the bull there sits a philosopher, on the philosopher's shoulder, there sits a parrot. What does the parrot say? – "Life, squawk, life."

There is in this locality, a misunderstood loquacity. What we fought for, is the tide. What it has left us, is more than enough. Come in closer, I have something to say – "We are all there already".

Mallarme – dream true, dream through, or just dream resplendent. Mallarme, are you the one that sleeps? Are you the one that has no dreams to speak of? Let us know, dearest Mallarme.

Hanging on by a thread. What is that that holds us on? Is it the mere thread, or something more profound? We seek something in nature, but what is that which we seek?

Mallarme – oh palace of wisdom, oh palace of content. There is never that which only goes backwards. There is never a fulsome acceptance of that which resides in the night.

Now that we have the motion – away, and through, and without fear, without the need to escape, only residing in something precious. Be the thing that lurches from one thing to the next.

Mallarme – are you the one who speaks of the betterment of things? Are you the one who knows what time the last train departs? What do we have, that no one else has? We shall see.

Intransigent and without care, the hills surround us, and nothing of our place in the wonder of things is here. So that we might carry our own weight, we beseech you, come.

Mallarme – is this the last of the fabric that we will use for making our own clothes with? I have never seen a more tattered garb than this. But that is okay, we will make it work.

Coming into peace, your final days were wrought with difficulty, Mallarme. What is about this time that can so inspire the passion of finality. There is nothing more to say here.

Mallarme, take charge of this, do not fashion a boat from oleander branches. Do not make a ship from the feelings of people. Do not, well actually, do, make us all happy with your presence.

Considering the template, we are not too far off the mark. Considering what has gone before, we are close to our wager. Be the testing of ancient ground, we will come again.

MALLARME

Mallarme – the sign of it is in the way we move it. Is it this way, or that? Is it up or down? Do come in, out of the rain, my sweet Mallarme. There is something here, we must revere.

Further than ever before, further than the sea's breath. Further than the molten trees that dance a merry dance. There will be time for feasting, when, once and for all, we send ourselves traipsing.

Mallarme, there is sense of things, that whistle's up to the length of things. It is a sense that knows no content, but lurches forward, never knowing when to stop, never really being.

And here, where larks are in the manner, there is something special, that cannot be denied. There is a likeness to the queen of ages, a visage that cannot be soon forgotten, nor replaced.

Mallarme – do you tense your arm before the event? Do you love the engravings before they are gone? What is this we have encountered – is it enough? Yes, and then through.

The signs of the work are finally here. It is a work of great beauty, and great impact. And when we have had the flames, and they have not burnt us, we will be again, like never before.

Mallarme – choosing our swords, and knowing when to fight. Knowing when to go, and when to stay. These are words that have the might of elephants at their beck and call.

The thistle, that does not let go. We will fight like this thistle, and know our adventure to be one of magnitude. Do not find us weeping, it will not suit. Do not find us in the rafters, we are not there.

Mallarme – sighing like it was a day of fits. Being like the ground, always pushing up. Being like the wind, and always being ready. Having the snow, and building a city. Yes.

The crescent moon, one that does not move. A further race to run. A new type of dance, one we will get used to. What we have never thought of until now. Until now. Until.

Mallarme – what is your accoutrement? What are the grains of sand that hold you together? What do we sense is the way, the way home? What comes from the horizon, and stays?

A light coloured thing, that does only feel its way to the top. There is a place we have yet to describe. In it, lies the power to be, and be strong. It will have the water of the stars.

Mallarme, gaining in momentum, will you swim? Will you swim that extra mile? There is a likeness here, that buries no turn. Let us believe again, it will turn for us, and then our weight will be lessened.

There are needs that the daylight can only be as one with. So what of us? What of the sheer adventure of life? There can only be the willing, and the able. There can only be what is left.

Mallarme - is yours the sound of drums? Is yours the hill that politely vanishes upon request? Is yours the sense we have that the journey is here for the taking? Have a load to carry.

MALLARME

The motion of the stars – is it our motion, one we have fought for? Is it the clouds that have solemn rite – is that what we have come for? There can never be a thing invisible to the touch.

Mallarme – do a trick, to see you through. Do what you say you have always done. Do what is in your nature, to do, and do well. Do what your heart follows, and what you have not forgotten.

Forging through, and in between, and a round, and a round. Do we know the distance from here to there? It is something that we have not known, but now do. Come, and be happy.

Mallarme – the last thing on our minds. The very last thing, and then, off to jump back into things. There is now a loose piece of land, that we thought was left for the gulls. Yes.

In this place, there is a farce. It knows no other way. It knows that the sound of drums is a curse, and a vestige of times bygone. See the semblance of things, they are a burden.

Mallarme, do you see the fruits of your endeavours? Do you love, so that love itself is felt? Do you crash to the ground, and then once again, rise, despite yourself? To be the one.

There treasure, and the map. The belief, and the surprise. The wandering, and the far. What we knew to be a chance at things, is nothing other than a way to be. Let us be!

Mallarme, singing and laughing. There is a tempest in the heart. It knows no soul, but has the pleasure of the dream to guide it. Let us dream, Mallarme, let us dream, and not fall.

Away, and in-between, and through, and seamlessly. What is lying at the cross-roads is a laneway of abandon, one that does not know when to sleep. Come, we must away.

Mallarme – do you smile at me from across the street? Do you know my burden? Do you know my sense of it? Please come and take a seat, and know your worth. This much is assured.

The rest are not at rest. The blue of sea, is not the green. What we thought was the action in things, is not the tide. The tide, is not the marrow. The wish, is not the wash.

Mallarme – do you see the closing in, as such, and know it to be a thing worthwhile? To be told a thousand times, is not enough. To be told once, can't hurt. But what is left after that?

The movement we see in life is as gracious as ever. Do not be alarmed, the test is nearly over. It tests your capacity to live, and to find a way through, no matter what. We will find a way.

Mallarme – come to the far side, it is a thing of beauty. It loves without the vestiges of life. It carries us without fear nor favour. It lounges on chairs of solid wood, and there, yes there.

Come and see what has happened at the cross-road. It is as if a miracle has happened, and will never be denied. There is, a mist that has enshrouded the place. But look, and see!

MALLARME

Mallarme – do you wander far? Do you examine things of priceless origin? Do you see the furthest from the best? There is more to say here, and we will say it, and then know.

And then, a mighty exclaiming, that does what it can to break the bonds of this world. In the middle of it, a solemn reminder that things can be difficult. And then, the weight is lifted.

Mallarme – do you hear the voice of a thousand nights? Are you the one who beckons neatly by the cry; the cry we cannot hear? Is this the way to go, so that we shan't go again?

And then, a new acceptance, to please the old. What's more, there is no time to speak, no time to rumble with unction, ramble with time. Give the way a welcoming home.

Mallarme, is this the way we go? Into crevices, into light, into the underworld, to see the night? There are now a thousand ways to be – all we must do is look, and low we are found.

The semblance of the trail is enough to sooth the injunction. Be insipid to the repour, and the noise of the garden will be no more. Send ourselves a champion, and the gate will open.

Mallarme – there are new things to polish, and new ways to polish them. And when we are through, a height that will astonish. Do not dream of it, it will not finish that way.

Wanting to see more, but feeling less. Do you catch more of the gold than is expected? We all want to know how. Watch the embrace of day and night, it will shock.

Mallarme – do you launch yourself under blueberries, under soil? This is where we hear our cry, and know it to be loud. Be the voice of the chosen, and yours will be a mighty vouch.

Send our missive to the outer place, and watch it come back with the markings of strange insignia. There is always a way back here, a way back to the unknown. Belief in things.

Mallarme, do you find yourself, with nothing but the sand between your toes? Do you find yourself now with only the lack to guide you? Is this the way forward, up, and beyond.

Making sure of things! Making sure we don't lose what has been begun. Making sure, even, of ourselves. Making sure. It is the crucial shard, and to be, of any great undertaking.

Mallarme – whisper your name to me, Mallarme. Whisper in quiet tones. There can never be any more than this, any more to pierce the bag of presumption. Be withstanding, it will suit.

Trudging through things. Boots on, heavy weather. What we see with our own eyes, and yet do not believe. What is yet to happen, and then, when things are most awry, peace.

Mallarme, do you see what we do not? Do you sit back, taking it all in, and then saying, "Ah, yes, I concur"? Be a troubadour on a troubadour's seat, and yours is a difficult one.

Never finding, never before found. What was once a loadstone, is now the remnants of a different kind of thing.

MALLARME

Be in tune with so much, and yours will be the chance to blossom.

Mallarme – do you believe again, believe in things unknown? This is what the treasure says, only more robust. Be in the moment, I implore, and yours will be a sycamore.

Come now, do not bend, do not send your soul to that place of anguish. Be the one to shine the brightest, and you have it all. I repeat do not bend, it will not be the thing that will help.

Mallarme, on the docks, perpetual wind. There is nothing left there, except sand, sand and a little water. Never has the foundation of a structure looked so fortuitous. Yes.

There are feelings that want to be, and feelings that shy away from the fence upon which we sit. Being languorous in a languorous land. Being uptight with the wind – we will escape.

Mallarme – sensing the euphoria, my Mallarme, there is a dip in pleasure, and then a feeling that is upright, and not uptight. Come to be my thing, will you? I will show the past-time how to run.

Giving it its all! Giving the fading light a new chance at remembering. There can be no second gasp, only the first will win. We must not think too softly, there are bound to be ants here.

Mallarme, what is this? What is this game? A game that purports to be another? There is a lingering now, one that does not know time. Listen to the wheel as it turns. It will come.

Shadows of unrest. Being diligent, but to no effect. Having everything we need, and then having it fall. Never before has the rain fallen so heavily. Never before have we needed so much.

Mallarme – the shade is not against us. The tide is like a falling leaf – back and forward. What we saw before we fell. What is it like to walk in reams of light? What is it like?

Heightening, and coming again. Heightening, and putting down on paper. What is more in line than this? What is more a-tuned, than this? What can we really believe in, anyway?

Forgoing the wreck. Be in form, but not knowing it. Being a vista in a vista's land. Holding on, but not knowing how. Being a rock, on a reef of sound. Never wanting to let go.

Mallarme, some to you, and some to your friend. Did you really dance the dance? Dance the dance fantastic? This much we say to you – come and have a natural spring.

Holding the banner aloft. Holding forth on things unsaid. A cherished mist that knows no ground. Being scrupulous, and knowing how. Being the rain, and seeing yourself fall.

There in the night, right there! There will be a party in your honour. Well done, you can escape. There is only what is left, and what is left is nothing. Do not sew a bow to your shirt.

Mallarme – do you sing before it is too late? Are you the rapidly closing speed? Can we be more than we had hoped? Is there something we don't know? Is there something?

MALLARME

Thinking of that something special. Nearing what awaits. Being lugubrious, but standing firm. Having the soul to keep going. Being in tune, and never falling off. Yes.

Mallarme, are you there? Is your hair, there? Does the fashion of the day, recite, in glorious numbers? Are you what we have come to see? Is this the way of it? Can we counter?

And then, without care, within reasonable time, there comes a sound. It comes in formidable form, and knows what to do next. It sounds to harbour, it sounds to the moat!

Mallarme, wing with us on this misty morning – wing with us, and see how we go. There are no mistakes here, only visions of what is included in break of day. Be kind, we must.

Forging ahead, without steam, without application, without the drying of summer tears. Can we really see the way there? Can we envelope ourselves in the wind as it comes?

Mallarme, do we see what we want to see, hark back to what we want to hark back to? There is more than the travelling of ages to be in borrowed acceptance with. Bring us home.

Thinking of the future, there is no fuss. Thinking of past, what a blast. There is no time to think now, of this or that, or anything in-between. Just time to be erudite, and test the strength of things.

Mallarme – are you the one who lives by the tree-line? Are you the one who hollers for the snake to dance a final dance? Can we even imagine what that is? Forthwith, and out!

The time it takes to enter the scene, should put us off. But it does not. And here, where the fire burns the brightest, a new star, one to feature on old news. Be the awkward acceptance.

Mallarme, do you dim yourself in touches of stone? Do you never renege a place amongst the places? Do you hold on to what is tightly drawn, and then come back again to wait?

Having to throw the whistle in the wind. Having to unload at the precipice. Nearing a spot which we take for granted. Being the one who carries the torch. There comes more.

Mallarme – silence, do not speak here, it is not aloud. Come and envisage yourself in your finery, and then jump in! Thank you for the carpet, it is a thing of beauty, do not hesitate to come again.

There are tempests, and then there are tempests. If one is flung into one, one must swim on the branch of a thousand yearnings. Come and be a positive to my negative.

Mallarme, swing, and joust, and be all you can be. Don't just sit there, the world is burning. Burning bright for the things that shine. Do you shine my Mallarme? Do you shine for the quick?

Having the patience, and seeing the formation of a constellation. Never a thing rang more true. Having the sense to see it. Holding on, and never letting go. You will not believe me.

MALLARME

Mallarme – is the donkey more than a stop gap? Are you sure you wish to ride? Being subtle, in a subtle land. There is nothing left to talk about, but that is okay, we will continue.

Sages afoot, and ranges on the lyre. Be a new beginning, it will be as if you could not ride anymore. Be the salt to your plain, and there will be a mighty insurgence in our world.

Mallarme - a thing worth knowing, is a thing indeed. Never before have we seen the likes of it, and never again will we see it. That is okay, for who would want to go through these things again.

Having to feel our way through. That much is written. Having to sense the marsh before we commence. Having neither the need, nor the desire – but please, do continue.

Mallarme, there is a sound we cannot placate. There is bush we must not strip. And then, out of nowhere, out of thin air, a burlesque show, that attempts to right past wrongs.

A here, where the layers of the cake stand in unison before the burnt out ravine, there is a stance that heralds so much, and takes so little. Be the way of it, it will liven.

Mallarme – something of you sings in me, but I am not sure what it is. Do you sound out things in ranges un-mutable? Do you have on your forehead no sign of disrespect?

There are places not to go – I have been to them. There are places that need no sharing, and I have shared them. There are domes on reading rooms that despair at the dark, and so do I.

Mallarme – there is something to say to you, when things are quiet, do not go down that well, it is not something I would do. But if you must, you must – that is the way of it.

Will you spread the news, Mallarme, oh soldier of mine? Will you linger tonight, as you have done on other nights? Not on the night of your Mardis of course. But tonight!

Mallarme – come and be a part of the show. Come and place yourself at the edge of the table, and jump! Be that as it may, we have a role to play here. And part and parcel, we will live it.

And now, a parting gift. We do not know what it is worth, or what it is even, but we do know that its weight is as much as ten elephants. Be the news, and be what you feel like.

Mallarme, can you see yourself at the masthead, being as belligerent as you can? Is this the way to be, with conscience in hand, and a bitterness at the reel. We will find a way.

And now, for something that will surprise. There is sand behind our back, and arches to our heels. And when we cast a net, we do so, not for food, but to let the living go. For life.

Mallarme – there are trees that do not sense themselves anew. And when they do, there will be a fresh branch to remember them by, and a solemn song to recant. In this we will be free.

Having said all this, it must be told that the embers that burn the brightest, are the ones that give off the most heat. And here, where we finish things in stages, a new dance, one to replace the old.

MALLARME

Mallarme – do you chance at it again? Do you feel the tinder at your cusp, and do you know its origin? Is this the way to proceed? Is this the way forward? We will see, for a second time.

Having the time bend, and knowing it to be a fiction of first rate adventure. Be in the middle, and watching on both sides. Here there will be more than a solemn march, more to go by.

Mallarme – having the glass, to take a drink. Seeing a whale, rising up for air. Seeing the morning, at first light. Seeing all there is to see, and knowing nothing more. Seeing what there is.

Finishing the trail, and believing once again. Having it all before one, and then motioning forward. Being inscrutable, this world of ours. There is nothing we can do, but march on.

Mallarme – a win! What is that? What is that you say? I agree, but cannot repeat what you have said. But that is okay, we all have our foibles. We must push on, to the next tundra.

Forcing ourselves through, and over, and beyond, there is something we don't understand – what is it? We cannot tell, but once we are there, we will know something of it.

Mallarme – come follow us, we have a mastery of the now. There is no dominion like it, and no tending to anything that is out of the ordinary. Be with us, and you will bark no longer!

A forest – that much can be said. A forest, and a waiting tree. There are times where comprehension is awry, but when we see ourselves anew, there is an affinity to be brave, and bold.

Mallarme – is this the way? Is this what you perceive in the mist; a certain foaming that delights in the motion of the stars, and all that will be? And now, we ourselves delight in things.

Hauling more than a carriage, the sweep of it is pronounced! And then, without care, nor rhyme, nor reason, something up lifts us, until the jack of all undermines the daylight and her hours.

Mallarme – do you see? Do you hear? Do you have these senses gladly? Well then yes, come, come for the sojourn to the winter palace. Here you will find us measuring things.

Saying what needs to be said. Doing all that needs doing. And then, without fear, there comes a semblance, a semblance of the rest and the departed. Be alive, Mallarme, be alive!

Mallarme – is this where we go, is this where we go? I cannot believe it! I am unbelieving. But just then, a new fight, one that requires the old. Be in touch, it will announce.

Catching a sight of the way forward. It is in blistering steel, and cannot be changed. And then, with sideways aplomb, a measure of the last of it comes clanging, clanging down the mountain.

MALLARME

Mallarme – have faith, have faith in things. They are here for the readiness, the readiness which is all. And now, we climb to that highest peak, and what do we see – but everything!

Catching a blistering speed – undoing it so that it might fall. What do you say? What do you feel? What is in the repertoire of the eye? Do you sense an unearthly surprise?

Mallarme – we swing, from this point to that. I have found the answer. It draws me ever onward. But what is the timing of it all? We know what is there, and what can be, finally.

Fastidious to the last, we will see ourselves in smocks of grey. And then, when we choose to relay the appropriate information, then we will have the last laugh on so much.

Mallarme, will you see again? Will you be the one to stamp on the edges of things, and never look back. To this, we say, a mighty, and encompassing, yes! There we have it.

Gliding through all that will be, and then seeing no more. Having the chance to really fly, and taking it by both wings. Have you had that dream Mallarme? Have you had that dream?

Mallarme – a thing to remember. There is no time for the lonely heart. Here is something we can live for, and only do out of love for the word, and the word only. Yes.

Catching goblins with a piece of string. Catching all else, with, well, all else. In the name of it, settle down, and be a-tuned to one last crescendo. Here, oh here, we will fight, and win!

Mallarme, are you the one to labour, and labour through it all? Does this mean that this will be last time we will see you? There are never things that bite quite like this. We will see.

On the foregoing chapter, there are prints, prints of how to go about things. And here, where we love all parts, there is more than a mouthful to swallow. We have made it.

Mallarme, be free, be free to muster. Be free to call this house your own. And then, when the light fades no more, they will come for you, and take you home. Be ready, they will come.

Oh heart of love, Oh soul of respite. There, in the chamber, oh there. There can be never be a time to explain the sea, and its motion. We don't want to at any rate. See us swim!

Mallarme, soul on soul, trepidation on the string of it. Do the strawberries taste like a wand? Does the life we lead never fall back, never fall by the wayside? Let us check things.

Gracious and strong, we stride forward through the night, not knowing where we came from, or where we are going. There is something obtuse, and something round-a-bouts.

Mallarme, to the last, the last ember of a fire that was lit a thousand years ago. Do you remember then, my Mallarme? Do you remember lighting that fire, and seeing it through?

Sending in the paper for a new work. It is one of epic proportions. A world poem, the great work, something to remember on your death bed. Something to wow the world with.

MALLARME

Mallarme – do you see the sea? Is this how far you have gone? Is this the road to follow?

Mallarme – you have given hope to high school teachers the world over – "I too can be a high school teacher, and be a great writer." But yes, your teaching suffered, but that was your focus, to be a poet, the likes of which has never been seen. You didn't suffer like Baudelaire, but you suffered in your own way. The pinnacle of your oeuvre, 'A throw of the dice will never abolish chance', was an early exemplar of the fragmented form in poetry, and it is certain, this poem attracts many readers to your oeuvre.

www.ingramcontent.com/pod-product-compliance
Lightning Source LLC
Chambersburg PA
CBHW020431220526
45464CB00002B/662